UPGRADING & REPAIRING PCs

STUART YARNOLD

In easy steps is an imprint of Computer Step
Southfield Road · Southam
Warwickshire CV47 0FB · United Kingdom
www.ineasysteps.com

Notice of Liability
Every effort has been made to ensure that this book contains accurate and
current information. However, Computer Step and the author shall not be
liable for any loss or damage suffered by readers as a result of any information
contained herein.

Trademarks
All trademarks are acknowledged as belonging to their respective companies.

Printed and bound in the United Kingdom

ISBN 1-84078-307-9

Table of Contents

See and Hear More With Your PC 105

Create a Reliable PC 123

Improve Your Input and Control Options 131

Before You Get the Toolbox Out

This chapter is an introduction to the subject of computer upgrading and repair, and offers some general advice on issues you should consider before you start pulling your PC to bits.

Covers

Chapter One

Introduction

If you are capable of wielding a screwdriver, you are capable of upgrading any part in a computer.

Given the pace at which computer technology is advancing, upgrading parts as they become obsolete is the only realistic way of having a PC that's capable of handling the latest software and hardware. Many people, though, are wary of delving inside the system case for various reasons. These include: a) ignorance of what lies within, b) fear of invalidating warranties, and c) fear of damaging the PC. So they take the PC to a computer store and put up with the inconvenience and cost.

However, it is a fact that the physical act of replacing a computer part is very easy to do and is something that absolutely anyone is capable of. This book provides you with all the information you need, plus illustrated guides on how to install every component in the PC.

This is actually the easy bit, though. Getting the right parts for your purpose and making sure they are compatible with your existing setup is a lot more difficult and is something that does require some knowledge. For example, say you are replacing the hard drive: these devices are supplied with various interfaces, e.g. SATA, ATA, and SCSI. All of these have their pros and cons, which make them suitable for some setups and less so for others. Which will be the right one for your PC?

Removing and installing parts is easy. Getting the right part is not quite so easy, and thus a major part of this book is devoted to making sure you get this right.

To make sure you make the right choices, you will find detailed descriptions of all the computer's parts and relevant specifications. This is extremely important as incorrect decisions may result, at best, in a PC that doesn't do what you wanted or expected it to, and at worst, in one that doesn't work at all.

There is also the issue of setting up devices. With some, such as a sound card, this is straightforward, but with others there is a lot more involved. For example, hard drives need to be partitioned and formatted before they can be used. Other parts require settings in the BIOS to be altered. Everything you need to know in these respects is explained.

Upgrades don't always go to plan and sometimes the new part won't work. If it's an essential system component, the PC itself might not work. To cover this, we provide a troubleshooting chapter that will help you to resolve most types of fault.

Is an Upgrade Really Necessary?

Before you decide to replace a component, make quite sure that it actually needs to be replaced. Some can appear to be malfunctioning when in reality the problem lies elsewhere, and others can be rejuvenated in various ways. The following are some typical examples:

Before buying a new hard drive for extra storage, try clearing your existing drive of redundant data. You may be surprised at how much space can be reclaimed by a good spring-clean.

- Hard drive performance can be seriously affected by a process known as fragmentation. So if you suspect that yours has a problem, you should always try defragmenting it first (see page 70). These devices can also develop bad sectors, which can be the cause of data loss. Running the Windows disk repair utility (see page 165), will sort this out

- When it comes to the speed of the PC, many people are fixated with the CPU – they think upgrading this part is guaranteed to give the system a boost. While it will to a certain extent, it is a fact that adding more memory will usually have a more significant impact

Devices that can be improved by a flash upgrade include video cards, BIOS chips, CD/DVD drives, printers and modems.

- Many devices have a flash upgradable chip (known as firmware), and most manufacturers provide firmware updates on their websites that reprogram these chips with a set of new instructions. Not only do the updates repair bugs, they often also add new features to the device in question. Check the manufacturers' websites to see if there are any worthwhile updates available for your devices before you replace them

- CD and DVD drives have a lens inside them that is used to focus the laser beam with which they read data. After a period of use, this lens can become contaminated by airborne pollutants such as dust and cigarette smoke. The result is inability to read discs, and even crashes and freezing of the PC. Before you replace the drive, try a lens cleaning kit. They don't always work but sometimes repeated attempts can be enough to restore normal operation

So unless you like spending money, and making unnecessary work for yourself, see if there's a way to extend the life of existing parts.

Buying Options

Having decided to buy a new part, the upgrader has two choices – retail or OEM. Both have their pros and cons.

Retail

A retail boxed CPU. The package includes the processor, heatsink/fan assembly, warranty and full instructions.

A retail product comes fully packaged in a printed box, and with a user manual, a registration card and a full warranty. In many cases, bundled software will be included as well. You will also be given everything needed to get the device into operation. For example, if you buy a CPU a heatsink/fan assembly will be supplied as well.

The most important thing, however, is that the product is more likely to be the genuine article – it is a fact that the computer parts market is flooded with counterfeit products of dubious origin (usually from South-east Asia).

The disadvantage of buying retail products is that they cost more.

OEM

OEM is short for "Original Equipment Manufacturer". The term is used to describe a company that manufactures products to be sold under another company's brand name. These companies (typically, big computer manufacturers, such as Dell), buy large numbers of the various parts, put them together and then sell the finished computer under their own name.

An OEM CPU. This comes in a plain cardboard box and with the minimum of accessories, i.e. none.

OEM products also find their way on to the open market and can be bought from all the main outlets. The big advantage is that they are considerably cheaper than retail versions. However, there is a reason for this: they are sold in a plain box with no manual or bundled software, and usually with a limited warranty (typically, 30–60 days).

Also, very often, they will not be the complete article. For example, a retail hard drive will include the interface cables. OEM versions will not; you get the hard drive but nothing else.

So if you want to save money, buying OEM is the way to do it. Just remember that you will get no instructions, a limited warranty, and possibly an inferior product to boot. If you want guaranteed quality and all the "bells and whistles", buy a retail product.

Sourcing Your Parts

Retail Outlets

Buying from a computer store is the quickest and safest method. If the part is faulty or you buy the wrong one by mistake, you can simply take it back and get a replacement.

Their main drawback is price. Stores have high overheads to pay and so charge high prices. Also, the staff in these places are often not too knowledgeable regarding the products they are selling. If you need good (and honest) advice, it may not be forthcoming.

The large chain-stores are the worst in these respects. Smaller, specialist computer stores are better and will usually offer good and impartial advice. Prices may not be any lower (they may even be higher) but the quality of service is usually superior.

Product details in mail-order catalogs tend to be sketchy. If you decide to go this route, check intended purchases on the Internet beforehand. For product specifications, the manufacturers' websites are the best place to look.

Mail-Order

The beauty of mail-order is that it enables buyers to compare prices without having to trudge around different stores. Also, sales staff are generally more clued-up than they are in stores.

The main advantage, though, is that prices will be considerably less than in stores.

The Internet

Just about every product under the sun can be bought online these days and computer parts are no exception.

There are many websites that specialize in this area. Two good examples are www.dabs.com in the UK and www.newegg.com in the USA (shown below).

Internet retailers are not above a few scams of their own. So don't buy anything from a site that doesn't provide a contact telephone number. Emails can be ignored; persistent calls can't be.

Goods bought online will be cheaper than anywhere else. A further advantage is that online catalogs usually offer much more information, e.g. product specifications, than mail-order catalogs do.

Precautions

Don't forget to back up things like your Internet favorites and your emails.

If you follow the advice in this book, you should encounter no difficulties as a result of any upgrades that are made. If you don't follow the instructions, or you inadvertently damage a component, you could have real problems.

One of these is loss of data. While we're not saying that this is likely, it is a possibility. Therefore, you are strongly advised to make a backup of any data on the PC that you do not wish to lose before you get started.

To do it, you will need a backup medium (a CD/DVD writer, a second hard drive or a Zip drive), and possibly a backup program as well, depending on the level of backup.

The simplest method is to go through the hard drive methodically and copy the required data to the backup medium. The problem with this way of doing it is that it is very easy to miss stuff. Unless you are an organized type of person, and thus know exactly where everything is, you may not back up everything you need to.

A safer, though more protracted, way is to back it all up. In this case, you will need a backup program, such as the one supplied by Windows (see margin note).

The various versions of Windows all supply a backup program. However, the one supplied with XP Home is not installed by default; you have to do it manually from the CD.

* *Open the installation disk and click the following folders: VALUEADD, MSFT, NTBACKUP*

* *Click the NTBACKUP file to install the utility*

* *To access it, go to Start, All Programs, Accessories, System Tools, Backup*

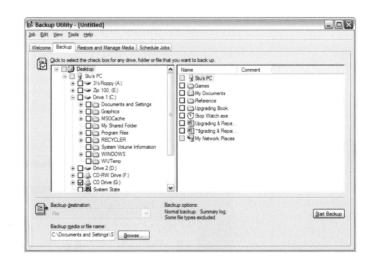

With this program (and others of its type), you can do a complete or selective backup.

Discovering Your PC

It is essential for the upgrader to know what's what inside the system case. This chapter identifies each component and shows where to find them.

One of the most crucial aspects of upgrading is making sure that the new device is compatible with the rest of the system; to help you with this, we explain how to get detailed information on every part in the computer.

Covers

Chapter Two

Inside the Computer

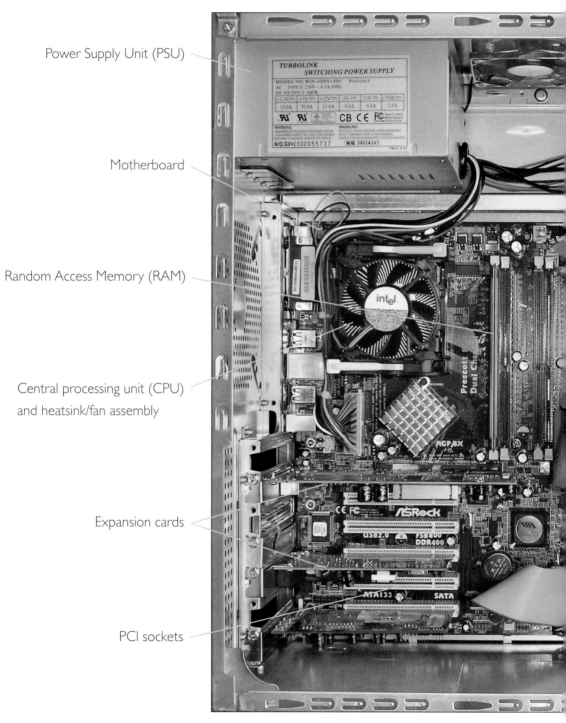

Power Supply Unit (PSU)

Motherboard

Random Access Memory (RAM)

Central processing unit (CPU)
and heatsink/fan assembly

Expansion cards

PCI sockets

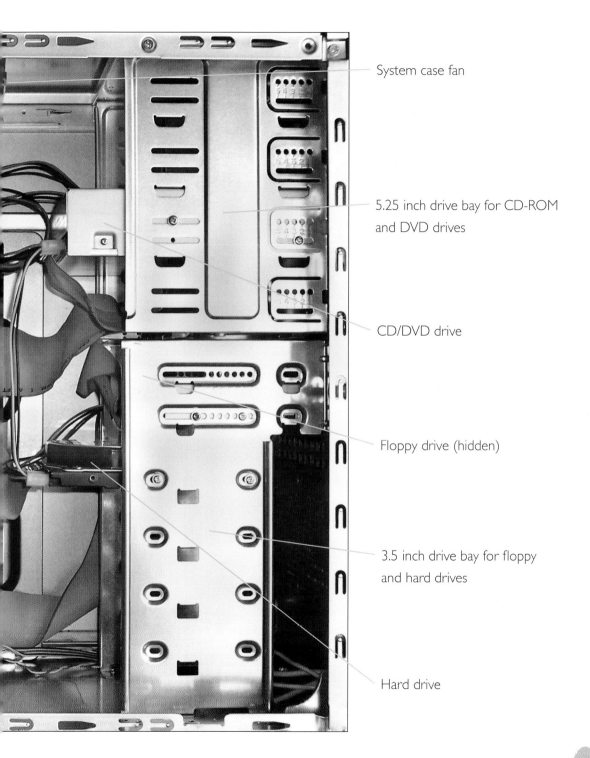

System case fan

5.25 inch drive bay for CD-ROM
and DVD drives

CD/DVD drive

Floppy drive (hidden)

3.5 inch drive bay for floppy
and hard drives

Hard drive

Outside the Computer

Power supply unit on/off switch

Power supply unit fan air intake

PS/2 ports. The green one is for the mouse, the purple for the keyboard

Power cord socket

Parallel port socket. Used for parallel port devices such as older printers, scanners and Zip drives

Serial port. This is obsolete but is provided for backward compatibility

LAN (local area network) socket

USB ports. USB is the standard type of connection now

Motherboard audio sockets. Pink is for a microphone, green is line out, and blue is line in

Video card VGA output to the monitor

Video card DVI output to the monitor

Modem socket for connection to the telephone line

Sound card audio sockets. The socket at the far left is a MIDI port

S/NO: 050467328

The Motherboard

Ports   CPU socket   Memory slots   ATX Power connector   BIOS chip

PCI slot   AGP video card slot   Chipset   Floppy drive ATA socket   ATA drive sockets   SATA drive sockets

Motherboard Sockets

Every component in a computer system is connected to the system's motherboard. To facilitate this, these boards provide sockets, or slots, of various types.

Note that AGP sockets are always a different color from the white PCI and PCI Express sockets.

AGP Video Card Socket

Video cards use the Advanced Graphics Port (AGP) interface. This is a high-speed bus that boosts the performance of these cards considerably. The motherboard's AGP socket provides the connection.

PCI Sockets

PCI sockets are used to connect other types of expansion card to the system. Most motherboards provide between three and five of these; some, however, may provide only one or two.

Unlike PCI, which uses a standard-sized socket, the PCI Express interface uses sockets of various sizes – x1, x2, x4, x8, x12 and x16. The larger the socket, the higher the speed at which data is transferred.

A recent extension of the PCI interface is PCI Express (see margin note), which offers much faster data transfer speeds. Increasingly, motherboards are now offering this new interface, usually with some PCI slots as well for backward compatibility.

PCI-Express x16 socket (for video cards)

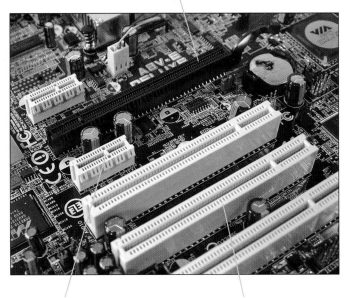

PCI-Express x1 socket   Standard PCI socket

Hard and CD ATA drive sockets are usually located on the right-hand side of the motherboard towards the middle. The floppy drive ATA socket is usually situated at the bottom of the board.

Drive Sockets

The computer's drives (hard, floppy and CD/DVD) connect to the motherboard via either ATA or SATA interface sockets. ATA has been around for some twenty years and is still found on virtually all motherboards. However, it is now being superseded by the new SATA interface. As with PCI/PCI Express, SATA-equipped motherboards also provide ATA sockets for backward compatibility.

This motherboard provides both ATA and SATA connections

Ports

At the top-right of the motherboard are its input/output ports. These enable the user to connect peripheral devices to the system without having to open up the system case.

Current motherboards provide all the ports shown on page 16, including the old serial and parallel ports. So if you upgrade yours, your system will still be compatible with any devices you may have that use these ports.

CPU and RAM

The PC's processor (the CPU) and its memory (RAM) are both located on the motherboard, and as far as the upgrader is concerned, they are the most important of its parts.

Note that in many system cases, access to the CPU is blocked by the power supply unit.

CPU

The CPU plugs into the motherboard via a large square socket. In ATX motherboards, the most common type, this is located towards the top of the board. Mounted on top of the CPU is a heatsink/fan assembly, which keeps the device cool. In operation, therefore, the CPU is not visible.

CPU hidden by the heatsink/ fan assembly

Heatsink/fan assembly removed revealing the CPU

RAM

Memory sockets are always situated at the top of the motherboard on the right-hand side.

Computer memory consists of a number of semiconductor chips mounted in groups on oblong circuit boards. These circuit boards, or RAM modules as they are known, plug into sockets on the motherboard, usually situated to the right of the CPU. Most motherboards provide several of these sockets.

Memory module installed in one of three available sockets on the motherboard

Expansion Cards

Most hardware devices are also available as external models. In this case they connect to the PC via its ports, usually the USB ports.

Expansion cards do what their name suggests – they expand the capabilities of a computer. They connect to the motherboard via its PCI or PC Express sockets.

The most common of these are:

● Video cards
● Sound cards
● Modems

The easiest way of identifying them is by their input and output sockets.

Video cards have either a blue VGA socket or a white DVI socket, or both. They are unmistakable in any case due to their fans and heat sinks

Another method of identifying expansion cards (assuming they are actually connected) is to follow the cable to the connected device. If it leads to the monitor, it has to be either the video card or the motherboard's integrated video system. If it goes to the speakers, it has to be the sound card or the integrated sound system. If it leads to the telephone jack, it has to be the modem.

Sound cards have a number of colored sockets, usually blue, green, black and orange. The sockets are often stamped as Mic, Line in, Line out, etc

Modems are small boards and usually have a single socket for connection to the telephone line. Voice enabled modems will also have Mic and Speaker sockets

Drive Units

All PCs have a hard drive and either a CD-ROM or a CD/DVD writer drive. Most also have a floppy drive. More recent PCs may have a CD writer and a DVD writer as well.

These devices are all located in the drive cages at the front of the system case, as shown below.

CD/DVD drive

Floppy drive

Hard drive

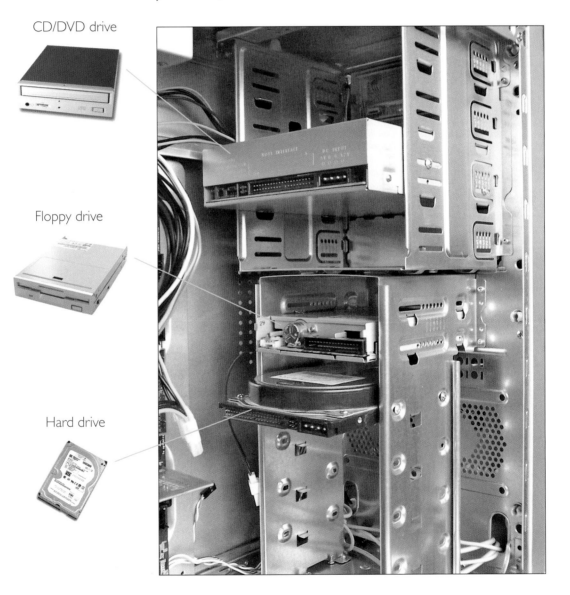

Upgrading & Repairing PCs in easy steps

System Details

When replacing or adding a new component to your PC, you need to know some relevant details. The following are some typical examples:

- When looking for a new printer to replace your old parallel port model, you will find that these devices now use the USB interface. USB is much faster and more efficient than parallel port, so it will be worth going for this as long as your PC is USB compatible. But is it?

- Your PC is running slowly and you suspect that more RAM is needed. Before you go out and buy some though, you will need to find out how much you currently have, and also what type of RAM it is

- You decide to flash-upgrade your BIOS. For this operation to be successful, it is essential that you know the model numbers of both the BIOS chip and the motherboard

If you still have the manual that came with the PC, all the required information should be available from it. If you don't, though, you need another source. Your first port of call will be Windows itself.

All versions of this operating system provide a system information utility (see margin note) called System Information. This will tell you many things about your PC, including the details of all its hardware devices.

Microsoft System Information

File Edit View Tools Help

System Information

Hardware Resource:
Components
Software Environmen

System Information
Microsoft Windows 98 4.10.2222 A
Clean install using Full OEM CD /T:C:\WININST0.400 /SrcDir=E:\WIN9
IE 5 5.00.2614.3500
Uptime: 0:00:01:28
Normal mode
On "C4B5A1" as "Stu"

GenuineIntel AMD Duron(tm) processor
96MB RAM
94% system resources free
Windows-managed swap file on drive C (3856MB free)
Available space on drive C: 3856MB of 4086MB (FAT32)

For Help, press F1   Current System Information

However, while System Information is undoubtedly useful, there are many third-party system information utilities that tell you a great deal more about your computer. One of these is SiSoft Sandra, a free version of which is available for download from the Internet (see margin note).

SiSoft Sandra is available at www.sisoftware. net. You will find four versions of this useful utility. The one that's free is the Lite version. Not all the modules are enabled with this version but the ones you need are.

SiSoft Sandra consists of a number of modules, each of which relates to a specific part of the system

There are many system information tools available for free download from the Internet. Go to any software download site, such as www. download.com, and type "system information" in the search box.

In this example we are looking at the motherboard module. As you can see from the size of the scrollbar, there is a tremendous amount of information available here

This utility is highly recommended and will give you all the information you need about your system.

A Faster PC

The components that have the most influence over the speed at which a computer runs are the CPU and the memory. Both of these devices are available in a range of models, each with specifications and features that make them suitable for certain applications. So it is essential that buyers consider both their requirements in terms of performance, and existing setup in terms of compatibility, in order to get the one best suited.

Covers

Chapter Three

Is a CPU Upgrade Necessary?

Do not be taken in by the marketing hype surrounding CPUs. In fact most home systems run perfectly well with a low- to mid-range model.

The usual reason for upgrading a CPU is to make the PC faster, and most people hope to see an immediate and significant improvement by doing this. However, it doesn't necessarily work as expected.

For example, say a 1.2 GHz CPU is replaced with a 2.4 GHz model; you may think that this will double the speed of the PC and that everything will happen twice as fast.

Unfortunately, it won't. While the PC will undoubtedly be more responsive, programs will not open twice as quickly, the PC won't boot up in half the time, etc. The extra processing capacity will become apparent only when an application that actually needs it is run. Whereas before the PC may have struggled to cope, now it will run effortlessly.

Before replacing your CPU, try installing extra memory. In most cases, this will make a greater improvement to the PC's performance than a CPU upgrade will.

So if your current CPU can handle your applications comfortably, upgrading it will make no significant difference to the performance of your PC. It would be like driving an Indy car in rush hour traffic – plenty of power but no way of using it.

However, should you develop an interest in any of the following, a CPU upgrade may well be what the doctor ordered:

- Video applications of any type. For example, movie-editing, 3D rendering and animation

- Computer Aided Design (CAD)

- Server applications

- High-level PC gaming. Note that a mid-range CPU will run most games reasonably well, but if you want to play them with all the graphic and sound effects at maximum levels, a top-end CPU is essential

Running applications like these on a computer system with anything other than a high-end CPU will have you banging your head on the desktop in frustration. As this is not going to do the desktop any good, you need to start looking at what's available in the CPU market.

The CPU Market

The CPU you buy will be from one of two manufacturers – AMD or Intel. There are others but these two companies dominate the desktop PC processor market.

Intel

For many years Intel CPUs were to be found in virtually all computers, and even today Intel still has the lion's share, particularly in the corporate and high-end desktop market.

Intel and AMD both manufacture high-quality CPUs. In terms of performance, there is little to choose between them. Therefore, for most people the deciding factor is price: here, AMD have the edge.

Like its rival AMD, it manufactures a range of CPUs that are designed to suit all pockets and requirements. These are as follows:

Starting at the top, Intel's flagship CPUs are the Itanium and the Xeon, both of which are designed for the corporate and server markets where very high levels of performance are required. They are also very highly priced. For the home user, they have little relevance.

Next up is the Pentium 4. This is Intel's most popular class of CPU and, along with the Celeron, is the one most likely to be of interest to the upgrader.

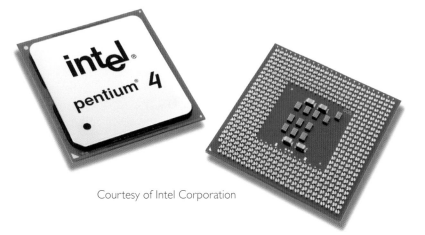

The main differences between a Pentium 4 and a Celeron are that the latter has a smaller cache memory and a slower FSB (see page 32).

Courtesy of Intel Corporation

At the bottom of the Intel range is the Celeron. This CPU is basically a Pentium 4 with a much lower specification. Even so, these CPUs are adequate for most purposes.

AMD (Advanced Micro Devices)

AMD is a relative newcomer to the processor market but, with their Athlon class of CPU, they have taken a large chunk out of Intel's share of the desktop PC market. This is due mainly to the fact that their products generally cost less than the Intel equivalent while still delivering the same level of performance. This has made them very popular with the PC manufacturers.

In terms of marketing, CPUs are classified into the following groups:

- *Corporate – the Xeon and Itanium from Intel, and the Opteron from AMD*

- *Desktop – mid-range to high-end CPUs are the Pentium 4 from Intel, and the Athlon 64 from AMD. Low-end CPUs are Intel's Celeron and AMD's Sempron*

AMD's top of the range CPU is the Opteron, and this processor is aimed at the corporate and server markets where it competes with Intel's Itanium and Xeon.

Next is the Athlon range, which is intended for mid- to high-end desktop PCs. The Athlon XP, which was introduced in 1999 and has been AMD's most popular CPU, has now been supplanted by the Athlon 64 (shown left). This is available in several versions, all of which are capable of supporting the latest development in CPU technology, namely 64-bit architecture (see page 34). However, the older Athlon XP is still widely available, and at a very handy price.

AMD's budget CPU is the Sempron (shown below). As with Intel's Celeron, the Sempron is basically a stripped-down version of an existing CPU (the Athlon), and offers less cache memory and lower FSB speed.

This CPU is also available in a 64-bit version, which is the most expensive in the Sempron range.

CPU Performance Ratings

Intel and AMD both have their own ways of rating the performance of their CPUs so that buyers have some means of evaluating them.

AMD

While AMD's CPUs have a lower clock speed than equivalent CPUs from Intel, performance levels are broadly similar.

AMD's method is the source of much confusion to buyers. This is because their CPUs run at a lower clock speed than equivalents from Intel while still producing the same level of performance (the reason for this is that their CPUs have a higher instruction per cycle rating, which means that they do more per cycle than Intel's).

For example, a 2.6 GHz Pentium 4 has a clock speed of 2.6 GHz. In terms of performance, the AMD equivalent is the 2600 Athlon. However, the clock speed of this CPU is actually 2.1 GHz, which is considerably less. Worried that if they advertised their CPUs at the true clock speed consumers would think they offered lower performance than Intel's, they introduced the performance rating.

So when you see an AMD CPU advertised at, say, 1800, remember this figure is not its clock speed – the real figure will be somewhat less. However, the CPU will offer the same performance as a Pentium 4 1.8 GHz CPU.

Intel

Until recently, Intel simply advertised their CPUs at the clock speed, which is not an accurate measure of performance. However, they have now introduced a rating system of their own. This removes references to individual specifications, such as clock speed and FSB, and replaces them with a three-digit number (735 in the example below).

The table below gives a basic guide to Intel's rating system. In general, the higher the number, the better the CPU's performance.

CPU Name	Number
Pentium Extreme	800
Dual-core Pentium	800
Pentium 4	600
Low-end Pentium 4	500
Celeron D	300
Pentium M Mobile	700
Pentium 4 Mobile	500
Celeron M	300

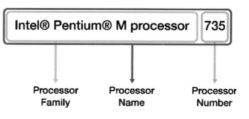

By itself, the number is actually completely meaningless. To derive any information from it, you will need to visit Intel's website at www.intel.com/products/processor_number/info.htm. Here you will find a list of all their CPUs, rating numbers and associated meanings.

What CPU Do You Need?

All desktop PCs can be placed in one of four categories: low-end, mid-range, high-end, and gaming machines. The CPU you buy will, to a large degree, be dictated by which of these categories your PC is in, or intended to be in.

An important factor to remember when upgrading your CPU is your possible requirements in the future. While you may not need a powerful one now, you may subsequently develop an interest that does require more processing power. For this reason, it makes sense to buy one with "a bit in hand".

High-End Systems

This type of system is typically used in one of two ways:

Multi-Tasking

Multi-tasking is where several applications are run simultaneously. Individually, they might not be CPU-intensive, but collectively they will be. The upgrader has two options:

- A dual-core processor. This is the best choice. Here, the CPU has two separate processors, each of which handles half the workload, thus giving the system a major boost

- A Hyper-Thread CPU. By means of some clever circuitry, these CPUs appear to the system as two separate CPUs, and to a certain degree act as two. However, they are not as good as a dual-core CPU

Running a Single CPU-Intensive Application

Systems running a single CPU-intensive application do not need to have a dual-core CPU. Here the choice will be a top-end single-core CPU.

Mid-Range Systems

These PCs tend to be used for a range of applications, some of which need a reasonably powerful CPU, and others of which don't. For example, PC games that aren't too CPU-intensive (not all of them are), office applications, email, and the Internet.

Hyper-Thread CPUs are effective only when running software that is designed to utilize Hyper-Threading technology. So before you buy one, make sure that the applications you need it for can actually make use of it. This information will be in the product specifications.

All of these will run very nicely with a mid-range CPU rated from 1.5 GHz to 2.5 GHz. Intel's Pentium 4, AMD's Athlon 64, and faster versions of the Sempron will be the choice here.

Low-End Systems

Basic applications such as word-processing, playing FreeCell, email, and web browsing require very little from the CPU. A 1.0 GHz model (if you can still find one) will be quite adequate.

However, if you tend to run several of these simultaneously, aim a bit higher: 1.5 to 2.0 GHz.

Suitable CPUs will be Intel's Celeron and low-end versions of AMD's Sempron.

High-Performance Gaming Machines

As a rule of thumb, AMD's CPUs generally provide better gaming performance, while Intel's are faster at more general PC applications.

For the hardcore gamer, there can be no compromises. The PC is set up with one purpose in mind: playing 3D games with "all guns blazing". To get the best out of these games in terms of frame rate (speed), and graphic and sound options, a seriously powerful CPU will be required.

AMD and Intel both supply a CPU designed specifically for gaming machines.

The two CPUs mentioned right are currently the best choice for hardcore gamers. By the time you are reading this, however, the situation may have changed.

Currently, Intel's offering is the Pentium Extreme Edition 840. This is a dual-core CPU with each core running at 3.2 GHz and having a 1 MB L2 cache (see page 33). The presence of dual-core technology makes it also suitable for heavy multi-tasking.

AMD's is the FX-57. With a clock speed of 2.8 GHz (making it the fastest AMD CPU), and 1 MB of L2 cache, this is one mean processor.

CPU Specifications

Now that you know what type of CPU is required in terms of performance, the next task is to choose one that will do the job. This means looking at the specifications, and the following are the ones that should be considered.

Clock Speed

This is the speed at which a CPU runs and is measured as a frequency, e.g. 20 MHz, which means 20 million cycles per second. As every action carried out by the CPU requires one or more cycles, it follows that the higher the clock speed, the more instructions it will be able to process in any given second.

A CPU's clock speed is an important indication of its quality but is by no means the only one. You must also consider its FSB speed, the amount of cache memory and any special technology employed.

You need to be aware, though, that there is a lot more to a CPU's performance than just clock speed. For example, you can buy a 3 GHz version of both the Celeron and the Pentium 4: the Celeron, however, costs considerably less and you can be quite sure that it is not going to perform nearly as well despite having the same clock speed. The specs below show why.

Front Side Bus (FSB)

A very important CPU specification is the speed at which it communicates with the rest of the PC; this is commonly known as the Front Side Bus speed. Going back to our Pentium 4/Celeron example, the 3.0 GHz Pentium 4 has an FSB of 800 MHz, while the 3.0 GHz Celeron has one of 533 MHz. So although they both have the same processing power, the Pentium 4 can transfer data much more quickly as it has a faster FSB.

Older motherboards do not configure the FSB speed automatically – it has to be done manually by means of changing jumper settings on the board. However, boards of this age are not compatible with modern CPUs, so a CPU upgrade will also need a motherboard upgrade anyway.

For the CPU's FSB to be effective, it must be supported by the motherboard. If the motherboard can't run at that speed, i.e. its own FSB speed is lower, data transfer between the CPU and the system will be at the lower of the two speeds – the motherboard's. Therefore, the system will not be able to fully utilize the CPU's processing power.

So before you buy a CPU, check that its FSB speed is supported by the motherboard in your system. To make life a bit easier for users, virtually all motherboards support several FSB speeds within a specified range. When the CPU is installed, the motherboard will automatically detect its speed and configure itself to run at the same speed (see margin note).

One of the main factors in the price of CPUs is the amount of cache memory. *This type of memory is extremely expensive and is why two CPUs of otherwise similar specifications can have a big price differential.*

AMD Athlon 64-bit CPUs use Socket 754.

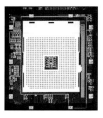

Newer versions of the Pentium 4 use Socket 775.

Cache Memory

Cache memory is an area of high-speed memory within the CPU, which is used to store frequently accessed data. Because this data doesn't have to be retrieved from the much slower RAM, overall performance is improved considerably. Using the Pentium 4/Celeron example once again, the Pentium 4 typically has two to four times as much cache memory as does the Celeron. Note that CPUs commonly use two types of cache – L1 and L2. L2 is slightly slower than L1 but is larger.

Other factors to consider include:

Compatibility

The CPU connects to the PC via a socket on the motherboard. However, different processors use different types of socket, so you must establish that your chosen CPU is physically compatible with the socket on your motherboard (see page 53). Also, be aware that motherboards are built for either Intel or AMD CPUs – they are not interchangeable.

Cooling

CPUs generate a lot of heat, and so must be adequately cooled by a suitable heatsink/fan assembly to prevent them from burning out. If you buy a retail CPU, this won't be a problem – an approved unit will be included. However, if you buy an OEM product, you will have to buy one separately. The important thing here is to make sure that the heatsink/fan assembly you buy is recommended for use with the CPU. If it is not, you could well have problems down the line.

Power

This will be a consideration only if you are buying one of the latest high-end CPUs. These devices draw a lot of power, so you must make sure that the power supply unit is up to the job (see page 126).

Technology

Intel and AMD both employ various technologies on certain of their processors. These make a considerable difference to both the performance and the price of the CPUs in question. We'll look at these on the next page.

CPU Technologies

When looking at the specs of Hyper-Transport CPUs, you will see that there is no reference to FSB. This is because these CPUs don't have one.

Hyper-Transport

Hyper-Transport is a technology developed by AMD, which replaces the traditional CPU Front Side Bus with an optimized interconnection system. The result is faster communication between the CPU, the RAM and the motherboard chipset, and as a result overall performance is much increased.

For the home user, the level of performance provided by Hyper-Transport is never likely to be needed except, perhaps, by those interested in a high-performance machine for gaming.

If you want a "Hyper-Threaded" system, you will need more than a new CPU. For this technology to work, it is necessary to have a Hyper-Thread compatible motherboard, and also software.

Hyper-Threading

This technology has been developed by Intel and basically "fools" the system into thinking it has two CPUs instead of just one. The purpose is to improve the PC's multi-tasking capabilities (running two or more applications simultaneously with no noticeable drop in performance).

Dual-Core

Dual-core CPUs have two processor cores on the same chip. Each core functions and processes data independently, and the two are coordinated by the operating system. However, a performance-limiting factor is the fact that a dual-core CPU has to share hardware such as the memory controller and the front side bus. Thus, a dual-core system will never be as good as a dual-processor system in which two separate CPUs are used, each of which has its own hardware.

If you decide to upgrade your PC to a 64-bit system, you may be jumping the gun. Although 64-bit operating systems are available, software manufacturers are not exactly falling over themselves to follow suit. The reason is that, as very few users need the level of performance offered by 64-bit systems, sales of 64-bit software are likely to be very slow, initially.

64-Bit Architecture

This is the latest technology to hit the desktop CPU market. Basically, a 64-bit CPU can process data twice as quickly as a 32-bit CPU, resulting in a much higher level of performance.

There are problems, though. Firstly, 64-bit CPUs are currently very expensive. Secondly, to gain the full advantages offered, software (including the operating system and hardware drivers) needs to be 64-bit compatible. So anyone upgrading to a 64-bit CPU will also need to buy a complete new set of software.

Note that existing 32-bit software will run on a 64-bit system but with no performance gain.

Installing a CPU

The procedure for installing the CPU itself is exactly the same for both Intel and AMD CPUs. The only difference is when fitting the heatsink/fan assembly.

In the following description of how to install a CPU, we will use an Intel Celeron processor (see margin note).

In the interests of clarity we are using a motherboard that has been removed from the system case. In practice, it is not necessary to do this – a CPU can be fitted in situ. However, with anything other than a mid- or full-tower system case (both of which give unrestricted access), you will first have to remove the power supply unit, as this device will impede access. You may also have to disconnect the CD/DVD, floppy, and hard drive interface cables.

The procedure is as follows:

Removing a heatsink/fan assembly involves nothing more than disengaging the fixing clips, which is easy enough. However, you may find that the thermal compound (see page 38) has "welded" the CPU to the heatsink. If this is the case, you may have to prise the two components apart with a thin blade. Just be careful not to damage the motherboard in the process.

1 If you are replacing an existing CPU, the first step is to remove the heatsink/fan assembly (see margin note)

Beware of your body's static electricity when handling CPUs. Purchasing and using an electrostatic wriststrap is recommended.

2 Lift the socket locking lever to the ninety-degree position

AMD CPUs have two diagonal corners and a gold triangle stamped on both sides of one corner. Intel processors have a gold triangle on the front and two pins removed on the other side. In both cases, the purpose is to ensure that the CPU cannot be installed the wrong way round.

3 Align the corner that has two pins removed with the corresponding corner in the socket

Make sure that the locking lever has been raised before you attempt to fit the CPU. This opens the socket's pin holes.

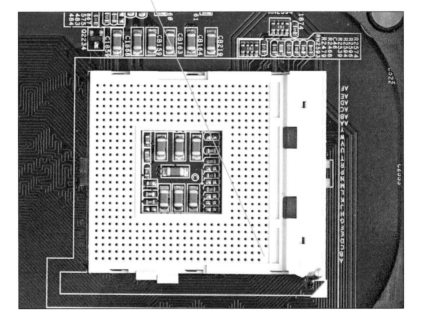

4 Drop the CPU into the socket

Unlike a RAM module, a CPU does not require any pressure when being fitted. Simply align the pins with the holes and it will drop into place. Note that the pins are very easily bent so a degree of care is needed.

5 Close the socket's locking lever

Make sure the CPU is fitted correctly (all four sides must be flush with the socket) before you close the locking lever. Otherwise, you will bend and possibly break some of the pins.

Installing a Heatsink/Fan Assembly

New heatsinks are supplied with a thermal pad in situ, as shown below. Be careful to keep your fingers off it as dead skin and oil reduce its effectiveness.

It is extremely important that thermal compound is placed between the heatsink and the CPU. This greatly improves heat transfer and if it isn't done, the CPU will soon either burn out or run at a temperature that makes it (and the PC) unstable.

Intel Heatsinks

Intel heatsinks are very easy to fit as they simply clip on to a retention frame that surrounds the CPU's socket.

If you are reusing an existing heatsink, you will have to remove the old thermal compound with a suitable solvent and then replace it. The compound is available from any computer store in the form of either pads or a tube of thermal paste.

Mounted on the heatsink itself is a clip assembly, which engages with the retention frame.

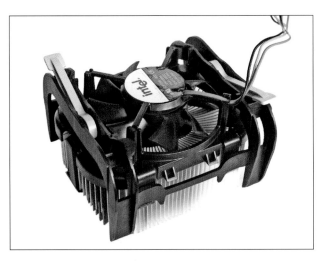

Align the heatsink with the retention frame and simply press down; it should snap into place

Aligning the heatsink with the retention frame so that the retaining clips are in the right place on all four sides can be somewhat fiddly. Once this is done, though, it snaps into place easily.

2 Swing the two locking levers through 180 degrees to lock the heatsink in place. Finally, connect the CPU fan to the motherboard

Don't forget to close the assembly locking levers; this is something that is easily overlooked.

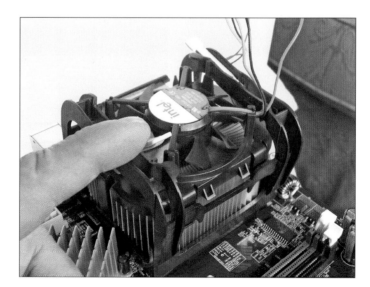

AMD Heatsinks

Heatsink/fan assemblies for AMD CPUs are a bit more awkward to fit as considerable force is required to engage the locking clips.

With AMD systems, the heatsink/fan assembly unit clips directly to the CPU's socket.

1 Check that there is a thermal strip or paste on the bottom of the heatsink

2 Align the recess at the bottom of the heatsink with the corresponding lip on the socket

When engaging the locking clips, hold the heatsink steady. If it slips about, the thermal compound will smear all over the place.

3 Engage the locking clip on one side of the heatsink over the matching lug on the socket

...cont'd

When forcing the second fixing clip into place (step 4), you may find that considerable force is required. If you use a screwdriver, be very careful – just one slip could be enough to trash the motherboard.

4 Engage the clip on the other side of the heatsink. You may need a flat-head screwdriver to do this

The CPU's fan power supply will be on the motherboard in the vicinity of the CPU. It is a 3-pin socket and is labeled "CPU Fan".

5 Connect the CPU's fan to the motherboard's CPU fan power supply

When is a RAM Upgrade Necessary?

When you buy a PC, it will come with an adequate amount of RAM to run the operating system and software installed on it. However, as the RAM requirements of both software and hardware increase with every succeeding version and model, the time will inevitably come when you no longer have enough.

If your PC slows down noticeably when running a new application, the time for a memory upgrade has come (it may also be necessary to upgrade the CPU but more RAM is the first thing to try).

The amount that you need depends on your operating system (all operating systems need a minimum amount to function properly), the type of applications you run, and the number of applications that you run simultaneously (multi-tasking). The following table gives a rough guide:

Operating System	Low Usage	Mid Usage	High Usage
Windows XP	256 MB	512 MB	1 GB
Windows Me	128 MB	256 MB	512 MB
Windows 98	64 MB	128 MB	256 MB
Windows 95	32 MB	64 MB	128 MB
Mac OS X	128 MB	256 MB	512 MB
Linux	80 MB	140 MB	212 MB

Low usage is defined as resource-light applications, such as word processing, web browsing, email, 2D games or data entry. If you tend to run several of these applications simultaneously, you should install the amount specified in the Mid Usage column.

Mid usage is running programs such as photo editing, web applications, multimedia, desktop publishing, sound editing, printing or scanning. If you run several of these at the same time, install the amount specified in the High Usage column.

High usage is defined as 3D gaming (particularly online gaming), real-time video editing, computer aided design (CAD), animation, 3D modeling, etc.

Types of Memory

Having decided that a memory upgrade is necessary, and how much is required, the next step is to see what's available.

There are actually many different types of RAM but the two that are currently relevant to the upgrader are:

- Single Data Rate Synchronous Dynamic RAM (SDR SDRAM)
- Double Data Rate Synchronous Dynamic RAM (DDR SDRAM)

Single Data Rate (SDR SDRAM)

If you have an old PC, it may well be using an older type of SDRAM called Single Data Rate SDRAM. You can establish this with a system information utility or by removing the module and taking a look at it. If it is the older type it will have two edge connector cut-outs, as shown below.

SDR SDRAM is outdated technology, so upgrading with this type of RAM should be done only if you don't want the expense of also upgrading the motherboard, and possibly the CPU as well.

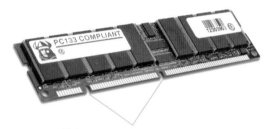

Edge connector cut-outs

This type of memory is still readily available in capacities of 64 MB, 128 MB, 256 MB and 512 MB. However, it has now been superseded by the much faster DDR SDRAM, which uses a 184-pin edge connector as opposed to the 168-pin edge connector used by SDR SDRAM.

As an older motherboard may not have 184-pin memory slots, upgrading to DDR may mean having to buy a new motherboard as well. As a result, it may also be necessary to buy a new CPU.

However, if all you want to do is add extra memory to your existing system, there's no problem.

Double Data Rate (SDRAM)

DDR SDRAM is currently the most popular type of memory. Essentially, it is the same as SDR SDRAM except for one major difference – data is transferred on both the up and down sides of a clock cycle, thus doubling data transfer speeds.

For the typical home user, DDR SDRAM is the recommended option. It is cheap and fast, and it will be around for some time to come yet (although a more advanced version – DDR2 – is now on the market).

As with CPUs and motherboards, computer RAM (whatever the type), is designed to operate at a specific frequency (speed). DDR memory is available in three main versions, all of which run at different speeds. These are:

PC2100

PC2100 DDR memory runs at 266 MHz and is designed for systems offering a motherboard FSB of 266 MHz. "2100" indicates that the module has a bandwidth of 2.1 GB per second (bandwidth means the amount of data that it transfers in a given time).

PC2700

PC2700 DDR memory runs at 333 MHz and is designed for systems offering a 333 MHz motherboard FSB. Its bandwidth is 2.7 GB per second.

If you want to turbo-charge your PC (and if money is no object), look no further than the PC4000 and 4400 RAM modules.

PC3200

PC3200 DDR memory runs at 400 MHz and is designed for systems offering a 400 MHz motherboard FSB. Its bandwidth is 3.2 GB per second.

DDR SDRAM is also available in two high-performance versions:

- PC4000 (runs at 500 MHz)
- PC4400 (runs at 550 MHZ)

Overclocking is a technique used to make certain components (typically, the CPU, RAM and video card) operate at speeds faster than intended by the manufacturer. This is done by the use of multipliers in the BIOS.

This is possible because manufacturers build in some spare capacity in their products so they don't run at "full stretch". Overclocking makes use of this spare capacity.

Both of these modules are aimed at hardcore gamers and performance enthusiasts who require their PCs to be as fast as possible. They are also popular with people who like to "overclock" their systems (see margin note).

Courtesy of Corsair Memory

A high-speed DDR memory module from Corsair

Double Data Rate 2 SDRAM (DDR2 SDRAM)

DDR2 SDRAM is an enhanced version of DDR SDRAM and doubles data transfer speeds yet again by having the chip perform four actions per cycle (as opposed to two actions with DDR). DDR2 modules are available in the following versions:

- PC3200 (runs at 400 MHz)
- PC4200 (runs at 533 MHz)
- PC5400 (runs at 667 MHz)
- PC6400 (runs at 800 MHz)

As you can see, in terms of speed, DDR2 carries on where DDR left off. Apart from this, though, it also provides other benefits, one of the main ones being that the voltage requirement is 1.8 volts, as opposed to 2.5 volts for DDR. This means that much less heat is produced. While this may not sound particularly exciting, in fact heat is one of the main limiting factors in PC design. Any technologies that offer at least the same level of performance as those they replace, but with less heat generation, are crucial to the development of computers. This is one reason why DDR2 will eventually supplant DDR.

Latency basically means a delay. In the case of memory, this delay is the time lapse between the CPU initiating a request for a piece of data in memory and it being retrieved.

However, it is not quite there yet, and the main reason for this is that it has a higher latency (see margin note) than DDR.

AMD is playing its cards close to its chest on the issue of DDR2. Rumor has it that they are planning to skip it altogether and wait until DDR3 is on the market before offering support.

Because of this, in practice only the PC5400 modules offer any appreciable performance gains. DDR PC3200 actually out-performs DDR2 PC3200 and is comparable with DDR2 PC4200.

You need to remember, though, that the DDR2 modules currently on sale are early generation modules; later generations will have the latency issue resolved, and will thus operate much faster than DDR does.

Another problem with this new technology is that it needs to be supported by the CPU and, currently, only Intel CPUs offer this support. If your system is running an AMD processor, you will not be able to use DDR2 (see top margin note).

A further complication with DDR2 is that even though it has been on the market only for a short period, the next generation, DDR3 (which will be twice as fast) is expected to be available by late 2006. If so, DDR2 could turn out to be a short-term interim technology, and as such, may not be worth buying at all.

Summary

Single Data Rate SDRAM is well past its sell-by-date and is found only on old PCs. Use it if you just need to give your existing system a boost in performance and have no need or desire to also upgrade the motherboard and/or CPU.

Double Data Rate SDRAM is currently the most popular type of memory as it is cheap and offers good performance. However, it requires 184-pin sockets and so users with older PCs may have to also upgrade their motherboard. PC3200 is fine for most purposes. For high performance, go for PC4000 or PC4400 modules.

RDRAM memory is currently available in 800, 1066 and 1200 MHz versions.

Projected versions will run at 1333 and 1600 MHz.

If you want your PC to be at the cutting-edge in terms of memory, you need Double Data Rate 2 SDRAM. This is the fastest memory on the market as long as you go for PC5400 or PC6400. Just remember that these modules require a motherboard FSB of 667 MHz and 800 MHz respectively to get the best out of them. Also, you will need an Intel based PC.

Double Data Rate 3 SDRAM is just around the corner, so if you can manage with your existing setup it may be worth waiting until it becomes available before upgrading.

Buying Memory – What to Look For

Having decided what type of memory will be suitable for your requirements, you need to consider the following factors to make sure you get the right module(s) for your system.

Quality

If you want a trouble-free PC, buy your memory from a well-known manufacturer.

Memory is a very important component and has a significant impact on both the speed and reliability of a computer. For these reasons, you must get the best quality that you can afford. While it may be tempting to buy a cheap module, you may well create an unstable system by doing so. Low-quality RAM can cause frequent crashing and system lock-ups.

The best guide to quality is the manufacturer. Unlike the CPU, where the choice is essentially between AMD and Intel, both of whose products are of high quality, there are a multitude of memory manufacturers offering modules at differing levels of quality and price.

We recommend you buy from Corsair, Kingston Technologies or Crucial. These companies all provide a high-quality product.

Form Factor

The form factor of a RAM module relates to its physical dimensions and pin configuration. There are several of these: SIMMs, DIMMs, etc.

Currently, mainstream motherboards accept 184-pin DDR SDRAM DIMMs and 240-pin DDR2 SDRAM DIMMs.

There are many RAM form factors, which means that you cannot just go out and buy, say, some DDR2 RAM because it is the latest technology. The memory you buy must be physically compatible with your motherboard.

The type you get must be compatible with your motherboard. For example, if your motherboard has 184-pin RAM sockets (which it probably will), you are restricted to DDR SDRAM. If you want to upgrade to a different type, you will have to upgrade the motherboard as well.

The best way to ensure you get it right is by making use of the online memory configurator tools offered by the memory manufacturers. The following example is from Corsair at www.corsairmemory.com (access to the configurator is on the home page).

The online memory configurators found at the websites of major memory companies are a very useful way of determining exactly what type of memory will be compatible with your system.

This lets you search by system or by memory module. For example, you can enter your existing system details (manufacturer, model, etc) and see what memory is available for the system. Alternatively, you can enter the type of memory you want and the configurator will show you a list of motherboards that are compatible.

Speed

While you can install a memory module of any speed in your system, it will only run at the rated speed if that speed is supported by the motherboard. For example, if you install a PC4000 module, which can run at 500 MHz, in a motherboard whose maximum RAM speed is 400 MHz, the module will run at 400 MHz, so you won't be getting the best out of it. Don't forget to check this out in the specifications.

The operating system also needs to be considered with regard to the amount of RAM that can be installed. Each version of Windows has a limit on the amount it will support:

- *Windows XP – 4 GB max*
- *Windows Me – 1.5 GB max*
- *Windows 95/98 – 1 GB max*

Capacity

The amount of RAM that can be installed in a system is dictated by the motherboard. Currently, most mainstream motherboards will support a maximum of 1 GB of DDR SDRAM. For typical home users this is more than enough. Only gamers and power-users are likely to need more than this level of capacity.

How to Install Memory

Installing new or extra memory is one of the easiest upgrades. Do it as follows:

Of all the components in a PC, memory modules are the ones most likely to be damaged by static electricity. So before handling one, ground yourself by touching something metal. Then pick it up by the edges.

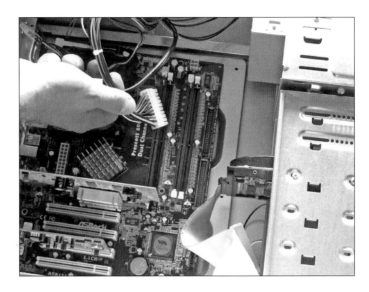

Disconnect or move any cables that are obstructing access to the memory sockets

When upgrading RAM, you will get the best results if you put the module in the lowest-numbered socket. Typically, they are labeled 0, 1, 2, 3, etc, with socket zero being the lowest. If there are no labels on the motherboard, the socket closest to the CPU should be considered to be socket zero.

2 Find the lowest-numbered socket (each one is numbered at the ends) and open the retaining clips

3 Align the edge connector cut-out with the lug on the socket

If possible, buy memory modules that are enclosed in a heat spreader as in our example here. This eliminates the risk of electrostatic damage.

4 Ease the module into the socket

5 Press down firmly at both ends

If the retaining clips don't close automatically, do not try to force them. You are either using an incorrect module or it is not fully inserted.

6 When the module is correctly seated, the retaining clips will close automatically

Create a More Versatile PC

To make a PC more versatile it is necessary to add to, or improve, its existing capabilities. As these are inherent to the motherboard, improving them will often mean replacing this device with a more up-to-date model. There are many factors that will influence this decision and the bulk of this chapter is devoted to ensuring that the upgrader makes the correct choice.

An important part of a motherboard upgrade is knowing how to set it up in the BIOS, and we explain exactly how to do this. We also show how to upgrade two motherboard components: the BIOS chip and system buses. These are upgrades that may obviate the need to replace the motherboard in some circumstances.

Covers

Chapter Four

To Upgrade or Not to Upgrade

There are three reasons to upgrade a motherboard: a) the existing one has failed, b) you want a more powerful PC, or c) to modernize your system.

Motherboards are complex pieces of circuitry that, essentially, define a computer system. Everything revolves around this board, but surprisingly, many people pay it scant regard.

Anyone intending to upgrade a PC is well advised to take a good look at what's available in the motherboard field. While we can only scratch the surface here, there are many websites that provide detailed analysis of the latest boards.

However, you should be aware that this is not the easiest of tasks as it can mean literally stripping the system down to gain access to the board, and then rebuilding it. Also, because so many other parts are involved, the potential for something going wrong as a result is higher than with any other type of upgrade.

These are two good reasons not to do it unless absolutely necessary. Another is that a motherboard upgrade may require other components to be upgraded as well.

The older your system, the more likely this is. Vintage PCs (ten years or more old) will be incompatible with modern motherboards in virtually every respect. Even the case will probably need replacing. In this situation, a brand new PC makes more sense than a motherboard upgrade.

With systems between five and ten years old, the CPU and RAM will almost certainly have to be replaced. It is also quite likely that some expansion cards (notably modems and sound cards) will be using the old, and now obsolete, ISA interface. Video cards, however, will probably be PCI models, and thus reusable.

In most cases, a motherboard upgrade means more than just replacing the board. Other devices will have to replaced as well.

A motherboard upgrade to accommodate a modern CPU could mean a new power supply unit as well. This is due to the high power requirements of these devices. It would be absolute folly to run one of the latest and greatest CPUs on an old 300 watt PSU: it would probably blow immediately, taking your new CPU with it.

The bottom line, then, is that before you do it, you should make sure there is no alternative. Clearly, if the existing board has failed, it's a no-brainer. If it's a faster PC you want, try a RAM upgrade first. If you need support for new technology, check that it can't be added to the existing motherboard in the form of a PCI card.

If you do decide to go ahead, there are many factors that have to be considered before you part with the cash. We'll take a look at these next.

Buying a Motherboard

Because the motherboard is the central component in the PC, replacing it with a different model can, and often does, have ramifications with regard to other components in the PC.

Compatibility Issues

All PC hardware needs to be compatible with the motherboard, in terms of both technology and method of connection. The most important to consider are the CPU and the RAM.

CPU

The first consideration with the CPU is physical compatibility with the motherboard. This means that the board must have the socket that the CPU was designed for. A quick look at the specifications will ensure you get this right. The CPU specs will specify the socket required – socket A, 478, 775, etc. The motherboard specs will specify the socket provided.

The next consideration is the motherboard's FSB. Ideally, it will be the same as the CPU's FSB. However, it's not critical if it isn't. The system will still work but at the lower of the two speeds (see page 32 for more on this). Again, you need to look at the specifications.

Many computer retail outlets supply kits, which comprise a matched motherboard, CPU and RAM. This is an option for those who don't want the bother of matching the parts themselves. Typically, these are available for low-, mid- and high-end purposes.

Another way is to use the system building guides provided by AMD (www.amd.com) and Intel (www.intel.com) on their websites. Just select the CPU you want and you will be presented with a list of compatible motherboards – it couldn't be easier.

The final consideration is the CPU clock speed supported by the motherboard. Most boards will support up to about 2.5 GHz; any higher than this, though, may well not be supported. Check this out in the motherboard's specs.

Memory

The considerations with RAM are similar to those for the CPU. Firstly, the module has to be physically compatible, and secondly, its rated speed should be supported by the motherboard. A possible third factor is the maximum amount of memory supported by the board. However, with regard to the latter, it must be said that most boards support at least 1 GB of RAM, so for most people this won't be an issue.

All this information is available from the motherboard's specifications, as in the example below.

Memory	
Number of Slots	2
Number of Pins	184-Pin
Maximum Memory Supported	2GB
Memory Supported	DDR266 (PC2100)
	DDR333 (PC2700)
	DDR400 (PC3200)

This board can support 2 GB of DDR RAM at speeds ranging from 266 MHz to 400 MHz

Form Factors

A motherboard's form factor relates to its physical dimensions and needs to be matched to the form factor of the system case and the power supply unit. This ensures that they are all physically compatible with each other.

The vast majority of PCs these days use the ATX form factor, which is available in three sizes – ATX, Mini ATX and Micro ATX. ATX motherboards are used in full- and mid-tower system cases and Mini ATX in mini system cases, while Micro ATX boards are used in desktop system cases.

A more recent PC form factor that was introduced in 2004 is BTX. One of the primary aims of BTX is to improve the level of cooling within the system case. This has become necessary due to the high levels of heat generated by the newer CPUs.

Be aware that if you decide to go the BTX route, you will also have to buy a BTX-compatible motherboard. All other system components are compatible with BTX, however.

If your system is housed in a full- or mid-tower case, you can use a motherboard built to any variation of ATX, as these cases are downward compatible, i.e. they have mounting points for all of them. If you have a desktop case, however, you will be restricted to a Micro ATX board.

Making sure you get the correct size of motherboard for your case is straightforward as they are all advertised with the form factor used. For example: ABIT KV7 Via Socket A ATX. This tells you the motherboard manufacturer (Abit), the chipset manufacturer (Via), the CPU socket type (Socket A) and the form factor (ATX).

At the top-left of the motherboard are its input/ output ports (see pages 16–17), *which allow external devices to be connected to the system. These are all standard with the exception of USB. This comes in two versions – USB1 and USB2. The latter is much faster, so make sure that your new board provides it. Note that USB2 is compatible with USB1 devices, although the speed gain is lost.*

Motherboard Sockets

The motherboard's sockets allow you to expand and update your system as and when required. It is crucial that the new board has the right type, and also enough of them.

ISA

If your system dates back to the late-1990s, some of your devices, particularly the modem and sound card, may use the ISA interface. As this is now obsolete, you will not be able to use these devices with a modern motherboard. If you have such devices, a motherboard upgrade will require them to be upgraded as well.

PCI

Currently, this is the standard interface for internal hardware devices. The only thing you need to check here is that the motherboard supplies enough PCI sockets for your devices. Most boards provide four or five but some have only one or two.

PCI Express

This is an enhanced version of the PCI interface that is expected to supersede PCI eventually. However, it is going to be several years before this happens. Current hardware, with the possible exception of video cards, is incapable of fully utilizing the extra bandwidth provided by PCI Express. So for the vast majority of people, this new interface is not necessary.

Even if you currently have no PCI Express devices, by buying a PCI Express enabled motherboard, your system will be future-proofed in this respect.

AGP

This socket is provided for AGP video cards. So if you have, or intend to get, one of these cards, make sure the motherboard has an AGP socket – not all do.

Note that the PCI Express interface also provides a socket (x16) for video cards. Some of the top-end video cards are now using this, so if hardcore gaming is your forte, you may want to make sure that your motherboard has a x16 PCI Express socket.

Drive

Your current ATA hard drive is going to fail one day. Buying a board that provides SATA as well means that you can upgrade to this interface when it does without also having to upgrade the motherboard.

The current standard interface for connecting drive units to the system is ATA and all motherboards provide this. However, the newer SATA interface is faster, and so it will be worth getting a board that provides both.

Integrated Hardware

Traditionally, built-in hardware was restricted mainly to sound and video systems, neither of which offered much in the way of quality and features. For example, early integrated video did not have 3D capability, which is essential for the playing of 3D games, and the sound systems could only handle the two nasty little speakers that manufacturers, typically, supplied.

Provided a high level of performance is not required, motherboards offering integrated sound and video systems are a good way for the upgrader to cut costs.

Today, the situation is much different. The sound systems now supplied with motherboards can support multiple-speaker setups, and the video systems have full 3D capabilities. For most users, these systems are more than adequate.

Quite apart from sound and video, motherboards offer a range of other integrated hardware, including: Ethernet and wireless network adaptors, modems, hardware firewalls, and RAID hard drive controllers. The advantages these offer to the upgrader are:

- Reduced cost. For example, buying a motherboard with an integrated video system will cost much less than buying a motherboard and a separate video card

- Increased expansion options. If some of your hardware is built in to the motherboard, you will have spare PCI sockets that would otherwise be occupied. These can be used for other devices

Technology

Whatever the reason for replacing a motherboard, the process of doing so presents an ideal opportunity to embrace more recent PC technologies at the same time. These include:

Bluetooth is a technology that allows short-range wireless communication between suitably equipped devices. These can be mice, keyboards, printers, scanners, etc. Currently, it is rare to see a Bluetooth-equipped PC. However, with the present trend towards wireless devices, its popularity is expected to grow.

- CPU technology, such as Intel's Hyper-Threading, 64-bit architecture, and dual processors (see next page)

- System buses, such as SATA, PCI Express, USB2 and Bluetooth (see margin note)

- DDR2 memory

Special Types of Motherboard

All the setups described on this page are intended for those who require extreme levels of performance.

Dual-Processor Motherboards

A dual-processor motherboard has two CPU sockets, which allows two separate CPUs to be installed. These act independently of each other and have their own hardware support (as opposed to a dual-core CPU, where the system's hardware is shared).

The result, not surprisingly, is a significant boost in processing power. However, as with upgrading a single CPU, this power will only become apparent when an application that actually needs it is run. Also, this type of setup comes at a price – an expensive dual-CPU motherboard, plus two CPUs.

Dual-Channel Motherboards

These motherboards provide matched pairs of memory slots in which identical modules are installed. Without going into the details, the result is a doubling of data transfer speed. For example, run two PC3200 (rated at 400 MHz) modules in a standard board and data transfer will be at 400 MHz. In a dual-channel motherboard, the same two modules will run at 800 MHz.

This provides a way of reducing, or even eliminating, the traditional performance bottleneck caused by memory not being able to run at the same speed as the CPU.

64-Bit Motherboards

64-bit architecture is the direction in which the computer world is heading. While it is going to be a while before it becomes mainstream, it is going to happen.

These boards are designed for 64-bit CPUs, which can process 64 bits of data simultaneously as opposed to the 32-bit capabilities of standard CPUs. As a result, potentially, they are twice as fast.

However, you should be aware that current 32-bit software is not able to fully utilize the benefits offered by a 64-bit system. To do so requires a 64-bit operating system, and 64-bit programs and hardware drivers. At the time of writing, 64-bit versions of Windows, Linux and Mac OS X are available, but 64-bit applications and hardware drivers are very thin on the ground.

By all means buy a 64-bit system; it will run all your existing software with a degree of improvement. This will be an upgrade for the future, though, as it is going to be a while before mainstream software is available in 64-bit versions.

Installing a Motherboard

1 Strip the existing board and disconnect all the cables

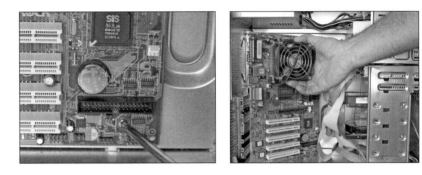

2 Unscrew the board   3 Remove it from the case

Remember to replace the input/output shield. This stops objects being poked through, which may damage the motherboard.

4 Remove the input/output panel shield and then fit the new one

Make sure a standoff is positioned in each corner of the board and in the middle at either side. If this is not done, the board will flex as expansion cards and other devices are installed. This may result in breakages in the board's circuits.

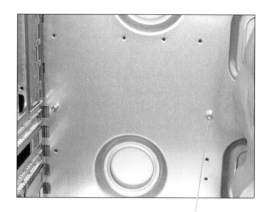

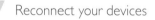

5 Hold the new board against the brass standoffs to make sure they align with the screw holes. If not, relocate them as necessary

Be sure to use the screws supplied with the board when you secure it in position. If you use screws from another source, and the heads are oversized, the result could be a short-circuit that damages the board or prevents it from working properly.

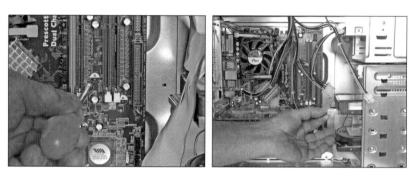

6 Screw the new board down

7 Reconnect your devices

8 Reconnect the cables for the case switches, case speaker, and LEDs

Configuring the BIOS

The key required to enter the BIOS setup program will be specified on the boot screen. It should also be specified in the documentation.

When the system is back in one piece, certain configuration settings in the BIOS need to be changed. This is done via the BIOS setup program, which is accessed by pressing a key as the PC boots (the key will be specified at the bottom of the first boot screen), as shown below:

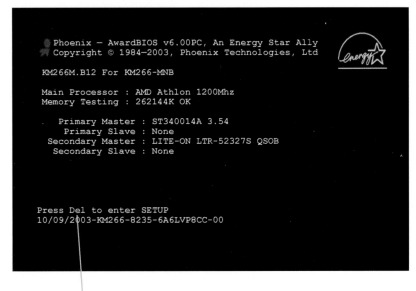

```
 Phoenix — AwardBIOS v6.00PC, An Energy Star Ally
 Copyright © 1984—2003, Phoenix Technologies, Ltd

 KM266M.B12 For KM266-MNB

 Main Processor : AMD Athlon 1200Mhz
 Memory Testing : 262144K OK

   Primary Master : ST340014A 3.54
    Primary Slave : None
 Secondary Master : LITE-ON LTR-52327S QSOB
  Secondary Slave : None




 Press Del to enter SETUP
 10/09/2003-KM266-8235-6A6LVP8CC-00
```

BIOS setup program entry key

Navigating the BIOS is done using the following keys:

To move around in the BIOS, use the Esc and arrow keys. Settings are changed with the Page Up and Page Down keys.

- Up arrow key – moves the cursor up
- Down arrow key – moves the cursor down
- Left arrow key – moves the cursor left
- Right arrow key – moves the cursor right
- Page Up key – selects a higher value
- Page Down key – selects a lower value
- Enter key – make a selection
- Escape (Esc) key – return to the previous menu

Date and Time

The first setting that must be changed is the date and time (assuming it hasn't already been set by the motherboard manufacturer). Do this as follows:

1 On the BIOS main page, select Standard CMOS Features using the arrow keys

Note that all the BIOS screenshots in this book are taken from an Award BIOS.
However, many motherboards use AMI BIOSs, which are laid out differently and use slightly different terminology.
If your BIOS is an AMI model, you will find the date/time setting on the page labeled Main.

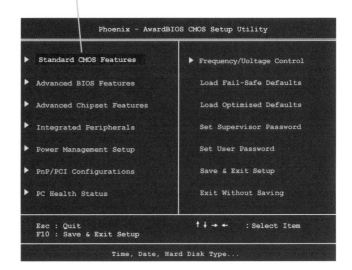

```
              Phoenix - AwardBIOS CMOS Setup Utility

 ▶  Standard CMOS Features          ▶ Frequency/Voltage Control

 ▶  Advanced BIOS Features            Load Fail-Safe Defaults

 ▶  Advanced Chipset Features         Load Optimized Defaults

 ▶  Integrated Peripherals            Set Supervisor Password

 ▶  Power Management Setup            Set User Password

 ▶  PnP/PCI Configurations            Save & Exit Setup

 ▶  PC Health Status                  Exit Without Saving

 Esc : Quit                    ↑ ↓ → ←      : Select Item
 F10 : Save & Exit Setup

              Time, Date, Hard Disk Type...
```

2 Scroll to Date, and then to Time, and enter the correct figures using the Page Up/Page Down keys

```
              Phoenix - AwardBIOS CMOS Setup Utility
                    Standard CMOS Features

 Date (mm:dd:yy)          Tue, May 10 2006         Item Help
 Time (hh:mm:ss)          11 : 32 : 9
                                               Menu Level  ▶
 ▶ IDE Primary Master     [ST340014A]
 ▶ IDE Primary Slave      [None]                Change the day,
 ▶ IDE Secondary Master   [None]                month, year and
 ▶ IDE Secondary Slave    [None]                century.

   Drive A                [1.4M 3.5 in]
   Drive B                [None]

   Video                  [EGA/VGA]
   Halt On                [All Errors]

   Base Memory                 640K
   Extended Memory          261120K
   Total Memory             262144K
```

Floppy Drive

We're assuming here that your system has a floppy drive; not all do these days. Open the Standard CMOS Features page as described on the previous page.

Those of you with an AMI BIOS will find the floppy drive configuration setting on the Advanced page.

Scroll down to "None", opposite Drive A

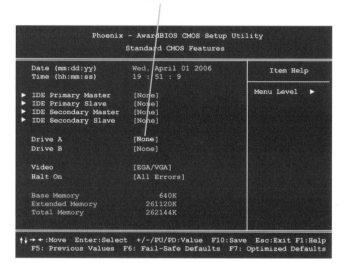

```
                    Phoenix - AwardBIOS CMOS Setup Utility
                           Standard CMOS Features

       Date (mm:dd:yy)         Wed, April 01 2006           Item Help
       Time (hh:mm:ss)         19 : 51 : 9
                                                      Menu Level  ▶
   ▶   IDE Primary Master      [None]
   ▶   IDE Primary Slave       [None]
   ▶   IDE Secondary Master    [None]
   ▶   IDE Secondary Slave     [None]

       Drive A                 [None]
       Drive B                 [None]

       Video                   [EGA/VGA]
       Halt On                 [All Errors]

       Base Memory                  640K
       Extended Memory           261120K
       Total Memory              262144K

   ↑↓→←:Move  Enter:Select  +/-/PU/PD:Value  F10:Save  Esc:Exit F1:Help
     F5: Previous Values  F6: Fail-Safe Defaults  F7: Optimized Defaults
```

Some BIOS programs automatically detect and configure the floppy drive. Not all do, though. If yours does not, you should follow the procedure detailed on this page.

2 Using the Page Up/Page Down keys, select the "1.44M 3.5 in" option. The system will now recognize the floppy drive

```
                    Phoenix - AwardBIOS CMOS Setup Utility
                           Standard CMOS Features

       Date (mm:dd:yy)         Wed, April 01 2006           Item Help
       Time (hh:mm:ss)         19 : 51 : 9
                                                      Menu Level  ▶
   ▶   IDE Primary Master      [None]
   ▶   IDE Primary Slave       [None]
   ▶   IDE Secondary Master    [None]
   ▶   IDE Secondary Slave     [None]

       Drive A                 [1.44M 3.5 in]
       Drive B                 [None]

       Video                   [EGA/VGA]
       Halt On                 [All Errors]

       Base Memory                  640K
       Extended Memory           261120K
       Total Memory              262144K

   ↑↓→←:Move  Enter:Select  +/-/PU/PD:Value  F10:Save  Esc:Exit F1:Help
     F5: Previous Values  F6: Fail-Safe Defaults  F7: Optimized Defaults
```

The USB setting in AMI BIOSs is on the Advanced page.

USB

In many BIOSs, the USB interface is disabled by default. Enable it as follows:

1 On the main BIOS page, select Integrated Peripherals. Then scroll down to Onchip PCI Device

When you have finished setting up the BIOS, the changes must be saved before you exit the program. Otherwise, they will revert back to the original settings. Do this by going to the main page and selecting Save and Exit Setup. Press Enter and then Y to confirm.

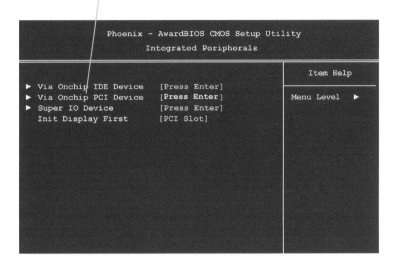

2 Press Enter to open the Onchip PCI Device page, scroll to Onchip USB Controller and set it to Enabled

Note that if you are using an AGP video card, this may also have to be set up in the BIOS. See pages 173–174 for details of how to do this.

Also, if your system has a sound card, the motherboard's integrated sound system will have to be disabled. See page 176.

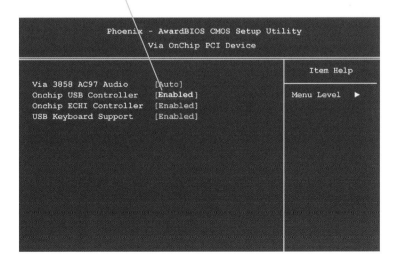

Upgrading the BIOS

Modern BIOSs are flash upgradeable, which means that the instructions they contain can be overwritten with updated versions. To do it, you need the update file, which is available from the motherboard's manufacturer, and a flash utility.

Note that many older BIOSs are not upgradeable.

The BIOS is responsible for initializing the PC's bootup procedure, and recognizing and configuring the system's hardware prior to the loading of the operating system.

As with every other part of the computer, the development of new technology renders the BIOS program out-of-date. Fortunately, modern BIOSs can be upgraded by means of a flash utility (see margin note).

But how do you know when your BIOS needs upgrading? The answer is: when you need to run software or a hardware device that uses technology not supported by the BIOS. This can be established by reading the relevant documentation. The following are typical examples:

- CPU support. The BIOS enables the motherboard to accept CPUs up to a certain speed, or of a certain type. In many cases, older motherboards can be made compatible with more recent CPUs by a BIOS upgrade

- Large hard drive support. Due to inherent limitations, older BIOSs will recognize only part of a hard drive's total capacity. For example, many current BIOSs cannot recognize more than 137.4 GB. So a user buying a 200 GB drive may have the frustration of being unable to use a third of it. One solution to this problem is to upgrade the BIOS

The most critical part of BIOS upgrading is getting the correct update file. To this end, you must be able to correctly identify the manufacturer and model number of both the BIOS and the motherboard.

- Bug fixes. All software contains errors; BIOS programs are no different. By making upgrades available, manufacturers are able to offer fixes

Flash Upgrading

Having decided that there is a need to upgrade the BIOS, proceed as follows:

1) The first step is to correctly identify the model number of both the motherboard and the BIOS chip. You must get this right – using the wrong upgrade may well render a BIOS chip (and hence the motherboard) unusable

Many motherboard manufacturers include the flash utility in the BIOS update file. So if you don't see a reference to one on the website, download the relevant update file. Extract the contents and you'll probably find the flash utility.

2) Locate and obtain the BIOS update file. This will be available at the motherboard manufacturer's website. You will also need an upgrading utility. These are known as "flash" utilities and will also be available from the motherboard manufacturer (see margin note)

3) Double-click the downloaded BIOS file (this is usually in a zipped format) and extract the contents to a blank formatted floppy disk. If a flash utility isn't included, you'll have to copy one to the floppy disk as well

4) Now create a boot floppy disk. See page 166 for instructions on how to do this

Some motherboard manufacturers now provide an automatic BIOS upgrade utility. Simply download it to your PC, click a button, and the upgrade will be downloaded and installed with no further input from the user. This is the easiest and safest way to do the job.

5) Place the boot floppy disk in the floppy drive and reboot the PC. When the PC has booted up, replace the boot disk with the one containing the BIOS file and the flash utility. From this point on, you will have to follow the instructions included with the flash utility as the procedure varies according to the utility used. Typically, though, it involves little more than simply typing in the name of the update file and its location, and then pressing Enter

Most upgrade utilities allow the user to make a backup of the existing BIOS instructions. In the event of problems, this can be used to restore the original BIOS settings.

A typical BIOS flash utility

Upgrading System Buses

A PC's bus is a communication channel that passes data to and from the computer's components. Think of it as a road system with the individual components all having their own addresses on the road, and you'll get the picture.

USB2 is the latest system bus for external devices, and offers data transfer rates of 480 MB/s. It is particularly useful for applications such as scanning, where large amounts of data are handled.

USB cards cost around $20-$30 US, and if you run applications that require high-speed data transfer, they are well worth the investment.

Different parts of the system use different types of bus, e.g. the front side bus for data transfer between the motherboard, the CPU and RAM, the ATA bus for the system's drives, and the AGP bus for video.

As computer technology advances, buses (and hence the devices that use them) become obsolete and are replaced with new ones. Thus, upgraders may find that their systems are not compatible with the bus used by modern devices.

Some of these buses, such as the motherboard's FSB, cannot be upgraded without replacing the motherboard. However, there are some that can. These are the ones that are used to connect external devices, such as printers, scanners, and Zip drives. Drive buses can be upgraded as well.

All that's necessary is to buy a PCI card that contains the appropriate bus technology and ports, and connect it to a PCI socket on the motherboard.

FireWire is currently the fastest interface, which makes it particularly suited for downloading video from digital video cameras.

Here we have a PCI card that provides two USB2 ports, and also two FireWire ports

This card adds the SATA drive interface to the system

Store More On Your PC

In this chapter, we look at the PC's main data storage device – the hard drive.

You'll learn about the various interfaces used by these devices, and important specifications – factors that need to be considered when buying a drive.

Hard drives need to be configured correctly before installation and then partitioned and formatted before they can be used. This chapter shows how these procedures are done.

Covers

Chapter Five

Hard Drives

Because they are mechanical devices, hard drives are guaranteed to eventually fail. For this reason, you should buy the best quality drive you can afford.

The hard drive is one of the components most likely to fail in a computer system. This is because it is a mechanical device that uses motors, bearings and other moving parts. Inevitably, these parts are subject to wear and tear, and will eventually fail. When a hard drive does fail, it is almost always terminal – these devices cannot usually be repaired. Any data that was on the drive will be lost.

There is more to upgrading a hard drive than the physical installation. They also need to be configured, and then partitioned and formatted.

Unfortunately, they also happen to be one of the more difficult components to upgrade. The physical installation is easy enough (just four screws and two cables – interface and power); what's not quite so straightforward is the configuration of these devices and preparing them for use (partitioning and formatting).

Furthermore, if the drive being replaced is the main system drive on which is loaded the operating system, then the system itself will have to be re-installed, plus any programs the drive may have contained.

The following pages explain everything you need to know to carry out a hard drive upgrade successfully.

Does it Need Upgrading?

There are three reasons to upgrade a hard drive:

1)   The existing drive has failed, or is beginning to fail
2)   You want to take advantage of more recent drive technology
3)   More storage capacity is needed

In the first two instances, there is nothing to think about – the drive has to be replaced. In the latter case, however, an upgrade may not be necessary.

If you've been using your drive for some time and have now run out of space, it could be time to simply have a clear-out and get rid of redundant data. The quickest and easiest way to do this is as follows:

Go to Start, All Programs, Accessories, System Tools, Disk Cleanup

The following are all signs of a hard drive that's on the way out, and need to be acted upon if you don't want to lose all your data:

• *Unusual levels of mechanical noise from the drive*

• *The PC locks up frequently*

• *File system errors (indicated by Scandisk or Chkdsk)*

• *Spurious loss of data*

2 Select the drive to be cleaned up. After a few moments, you will be presented with a list of files that can be safely deleted. Make your selection by checking the appropriate boxes and then click OK

Those of you running versions of Windows from Me onwards have a utility known as System Restore. This is used to restore the system to a previous state in the event of problems, and it works by taking a snapshot of the system at periodic intervals and saving it as a file. These files can be huge, and a number of them can occupy several gigabytes of hard drive space.

Clicking the More Options tab gives you three more options:

1)   The removal of Windows components that are not used
2)   The removal of third-party programs that are not used
3)   The deletion of System Restore files (see margin note)

Work through these and delete as much stuff as you can.

This should free up enough hard drive space to cover most purposes, particularly if you had a lot of System Restore files.

If lack of storage space is the issue, consider buying a DVD writer (see pages 97–98) rather than upgrading the hard drive. DVD discs hold up to 8.5 GB of data and provide an ideal means of archiving your files.

However, if you need room for graphics, you may still not have enough; these use a huge amount of disk capacity. For example, one high-resolution image from a digital camera will be around 2 MB in size, and a full-length movie (depending on the resolution and level of compression) can be 1 GB.

Fragmentation

Another issue that must be considered is that of fragmentation. This is a process in which files saved to a drive are split up, i.e. fragmented, into smaller pieces and saved on different locations on the drive. This means that the drive's read/write heads have to hunt about for a file's fragments and re-assemble them into the complete file before presenting it to the user. This is a time consuming process, the effect of which is that the file takes a lot longer to open. The user may observe the system running slowly and may conclude that the CPU and/or RAM (or even the hard drive itself) needs upgrading, when in reality all that's required is simple maintenance.

So before upgrading any component in an attempt to speed up your system, try defragmenting the hard drive first. This procedure reverses the fragmentation process and will give the system a considerable boost. Do it as follows:

When defragmenting a hard drive, make sure there are no programs running other than the defragmenting utility itself. Other programs can interfere with the process and cause it to keep restarting.

1 Go to Start, All Programs, Accessories, System Tools, Disk Defragmenter. Select Drive C and click Defragment

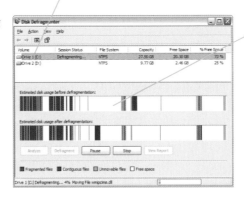

2 The defragmentation procedure in process. Note that this can take an hour or more to complete, depending on the size of the drive

Internal Hard Drives

Having made the decision to upgrade your hard drive, your next decision is what type of drive to go for.

These devices are classified by the interface used, for example a SATA drive runs from the SATA interface. Internal hard drives use one of three interfaces: ATA, SATA or SCSI. External models, which we look at on page 73, use either the USB or the FireWire interface.

ATA

The ATA interface can be confusing for the unitiated as it goes by several names. When you see a drive described by any of the following, it is an ATA drive:

- *IDE*
- *EIDE*
- *DMA*
- *UDMA*

The ATA (Advanced Technology Attachment) standard originated way back in 1986 and has since undergone many improvements, which have increased the speed and size of the drives that it can support. The latest version is ATA-7, which supports data transfer speeds of up to 133 MB/s. However, due to the recent introduction of the SATA interface (below), this is likely to be the last update for ATA. In other words, it is now on the way out.

SATA

SATA (Serial ATA) is a development of the ATA interface and provides several major improvements. These include:

Unlike ATA, where two separate drives can be connected to a single socket, SATA allows only one.

- Data transfer speeds. The first generation of SATA, SATA1, had a data transfer speed of 150 MB/s, compared with a maximum of 133 MB/s for ATA. The current SATA generation, SATA2, transfers data at 300 MB/s, and future generations are expected to offer at least 600 MB/s

- Hot-swapping capabilities. SATA drives can be connected and disconnected while the PC is running, unlike ATA drives, which require the PC to be powered off before this can be done

- Power requirements. SATA drives have a lower power requirement than ATA drives, which in turn means that less heat is generated

- Setting up. SATA drives do not need to be configured as master or slave as do ATA drives (see page 77). However, they do need to be partitioned and formatted.

● Improved airflow. SATA drives use a slimline interface cable that offers much less resistance to airflow than the 80-wire ribbon cables used by ATA drives

SATA cable   ATA ribbon cable

SCSI hard drives have a high rotational speed (typically, 15,000 rpm). Side effects of this are higher noise and heat emission levels. Also, maximum storage capacities are less than with ATA and SATA drives.

SCSI

SCSI (Small Computer System Interface) is actually a system interface that can be used with many types of device – it is not restricted for use with hard drives.

SCSI hard drives provide fast data transfer speeds (320 MB/s), high levels of performance and great reliability. These qualities make them ideal for use in server and corporate environments, which is in fact where they are normally seen.

They do have some disadvantages, though. Firstly, they are very expensive (costing, typically, four times as much as an ATA/SATA drive of similar capacity).

If you wish to take advantage of the high performance levels and reliability offered by SCSI hard drives, you will need to add the SCSI interface to your system.

Secondly, as very few motherboards have native support for SCSI, it is usually necessary to install a SCSI adaptor card, as shown here. This adds further to the expense. However, once fitted, the adaptor card allows you to run other SCSI devices as well, thus increasing the system's expansion options.

External Hard Drives

External hard drives use either the USB or the FireWire interface, and this provides one of the main benefits of these devices: ease of installation – simply plug them in and they are ready to go. Furthermore, unlike internal models, they are supplied pre-partitioned and formatted, and do not require jumper configuration (see page 77).

For those of you who like to keep things simple but need more space, an external hard drive is the way to go.

Other advantages include:

- Easy transportation of data. Simply unplug from one PC and connect to another

- Data transfer speed. USB and FireWire are both high-speed interfaces (480 MB/s for USB and up to 800 MB/s for FireWire)

- Higher capacities. Internal drives are limited in terms of physical size by the constraints of the system case, which in turn limits their maximum storage capacity, currently to around 500 GB. External models have no such limits and so are available with capacities of 1 GB and over

However, they do have some disadvantages and these are:

External hard drives are much more expensive then internal drives.

- Because they have to be supplied in a robust case and, in some instances, with a separate power supply, they cost much more than internal models of equivalent capacity

- They cannot be used as the main system drive, i.e. you can't install the operating system on them. Thus, they are restricted to additional storage purposes

Hard Drive Capacity Limitations

The DDO method of overcoming BIOS hard drive limitations is not as good as upgrading the BIOS and can be the cause of several problems. These include:

- *Operating system issues – the installation of a new operating system, or setting up of a dual-boot system can cause bootup and data loss problems*

- *DDO can be very difficult to remove from a system and may require the use of a special program*

- *Compatibility issues – if you have two hard drives in your system, each from a different manufacturer, you may have problems getting both to work*

Having said all this, if you don't do anything out of the ordinary with your PC, DDO will be OK.

Those of you with an old PC need to be aware of a problem that is caused by older BIOS chips – your system may not recognize the full capacity of a modern hard drive. This is due to limitations inherent in the BIOS and, in some cases, the operating system.

Unfortunately, we don't have room here to go into the technical reason for this (it's not very interesting, anyway) but it comes down to the fact that when the ATA drive interface was developed, the design of hard disk structures, access routines, and operating systems did not take into account the amazing increase in drive storage capacity that was to follow. As the various limitations became apparent (528 MB, 2.1 GB, 4.2 GB, 8.4 GB, 32 GB and 137 GB), various methods of overcoming them were developed.

The easiest and most commonly used of these is the Dynamic Disk Overlay (DDO) method. Basically, this overrides the part of the BIOS instructions that address the issue of hard drive translation, and thus enables the full capacity of a drive to be recognized. A DDO program is usually provided by hard drive manufacturers (assuming you buy a retail version – if you buy an OEM version, you will have to download the program from the manufacturer's website). However, there are issues with DDO (see top margin note) that make it a less than ideal method.

A much better way, if it's possible, is to flash upgrade the BIOS (see pages 64–65). This provides a permanent solution that has no software ramifications, unlike the DDO method. However, the BIOS chips on really old systems cannot be upgraded. For these, DDO provides the only realistic solution.

The latest drive capacity limitation is 137 GB. To overcome this requires not only the BIOS issue to be addressed, but also the operating system to be modified to support 48-bit hard drive addressing. The solution is as follows:

Another method is to install an ATA hard drive controller card. This replaces the ATA controller on the motherboard, and in doing so, eliminates any BIOS size restrictions. These cards are cheap (typically, around $20 US) and provide a much better solution than DDO.

- Windows XP – install Service Pack 2
- Windows 2000 – install Service Pack 3
- Windows 95sr2/98/Me/NT – install a 48-bit controller card

Hard Drive Specifications

It is essential that you buy a good quality hard drive and the way to ensure that you do is to look at the relevant specifications. The best place to find these is the manufacturer's or seller's website. A typical example is shown below:

As with all parts of a PC, the manufacturer's website is the best place to find detailed specifications.

Specifications	
Capacity	80 GB
External Data Transfer Rate	150 MBps
Internal Data Transfer Rate	760 Mbit/s
Seek Time	8 ms
Buffer Size	8 MB
Interface	Serial ATA
Rotational Speed	7200 rpm

Looking at these from the top, we have:

Capacity

Hard drive capacity is measured in gigabytes (GB) and is the specification (often, the only specification) most commonly looked at by buyers. We cannot tell you what you need in this respect – it depends entirely on what you use the PC for. However, when making your decision, bear the following in mind:

Don't forget to factor in the possibility of one day discovering a new use for your PC that may require a large amount of disk space.

- Consider not just your present requirements, but also those of the future. Whereas, years ago, lack of hard drive capacity was a limiting factor in software design, this is no longer the case and software applications can now be enormous in size

- Hard drives do not perform at their best when they are at, or close to, maximum capacity – data transfer rates drop. As a rough guide, thirty percent of their capacity should be unused in order to achieve maximum performance

- Graphics files consume vast amounts of disk space

External Data Transfer Rate

This is the speed at which data is transferred from the drive to the system, and vice versa. The difference between the various versions of ATA (100 to 133 MB/s) and SATA1 (150 MB/s) is marginal and really isn't an issue.

Currently, SATA2 provides the fastest external data transfer speed for internal drives. For external drives, FireWire is the fastest.

Some manufacturers specify a drive's Seek Time and others specify Access Time. Whichever, a figure of around 8 ms is good.

Look for a rotational speed of 7200 rpm. Cheaper drives will have one of 5400. SCSI drives offer rotational speeds between 10,000 and 15,000.

However, the difference between ATA/SATA1, and SATA2 (300 MB/s) and SCSI (320 MB/s) is considerable.

Internal Data Transfer Rate

This is the speed at which a drive can write and read data to and from its disks, and is a very important indication of its performance.

Seek/Access Time

This is a measure of the time required for the drive's read/write heads to move between tracks over the surfaces of the disks. Note that Seek Time and Access Time are actually different specs but are close enough to be considered the same.

Buffer Size

The buffer is an area of high-speed memory that is used to store frequently accessed data in order to improve performance. The size is not critical. For most users, 2 MB is adequate. Power users, however, will benefit from a higher buffer size.

Interface

The type of interface used to connect the drive to the system (see pages 71-72).

Rotational Speed

This is a measure of how fast a drive's disk platters spin and is a very important specification, as it directly affects the speed at which the drive reads and writes data. The faster the rotational speed, the better the drive's performance.

The following table sums up typical specifications for hard drives aimed at different sections of the market.

	Low End	Mid Range	High End
Drive Type	ATA	SATA1	SATA2/SCSI
External Data Transfer Rate	100–133	150	300–320
Internal Data Transfer Rate	400–600	600–750	800–900
Seek/Access Time	12	8.5	3.6
Rotational Speed	5400	7200	7200–15,000
Buffer Size	2	2	8

Configuring an ATA Hard Drive

The ATA interface can handle two drives simultaneously. In this situation, an order of preference must be set in which one drive is the master and the other the slave.

To facilitate this, hard drives are supplied with a jumper block at the rear, which has four pairs of pins, each pair providing a different configuration. A 2-pin jumper is used to select the one required.

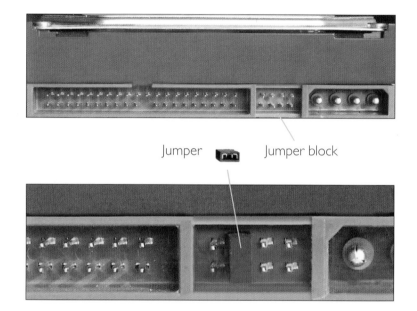

Jumper   Jumper block

If you are just replacing the existing drive, all you have to do is confirm that the jumper is in the correct position to set the drive as the master. While most drives are supplied with this as the default setting, you have to check (the jumper could have worked loose during transit, for example).

To enable users to place the jumpers correctly, most drives have a jumper setting table printed on the case, as shown left.

If you are installing a second drive, the drive on which the operating system is installed should be set as the master; this will give the best results. It should be the faster or newer of the two.

Installing an ATA Hard Drive

Hard drives are delicate devices and do not respond well to knocks and being dropped.

| Move the floppy drive cable out of the way

2 Slide the drive into position

If you fit the drive upside down, it won't work for long. The 4-pin power socket should be on the right.

3 Secure the drive with the screws supplied

80-pin ATA interface cables are keyed to make sure they are fitted the right way round. If the plug won't fit one way, try the other.

4 Connect the black end of the drive interface cable to the ATA socket

5 Connect up the power supply

The motherboard will have two ATA sockets – one for the hard drive (colored) and one for the CD drive (black). Make sure you connect the hard drive to the colored socket.

6 Locate the colored ATA socket on the motherboard

7 Connect the other end of the interface cable (with the colored plug) to the motherboard

Don't leave the interface cable hanging loosely in the case; this will obstruct the flow of air. Fold up any slack and push it out of the way as far as possible.

8 Job done. All that remains now is to tidy up (see margin note)

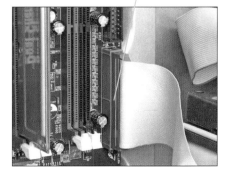

Installing a Second ATA Hard Drive

Leaving a space between hard drives prevents heat from one affecting the other. It's not critical but if the space is there, use it.

Slide the drive into the next but one bay from the main drive (see margin note)

The slave connector is in the middle of the interface cable, as shown below.

2 Secure the drive with the supplied screws

3 Connect the gray slave interface plug to the drive

Remember to configure the drive as the slave by means of the appropriate jumper setting.

4 Connect a power plug

Installing a SATA Hard Drive

This is exactly the same procedure as for an ATA drive. The only difference is that SATA drives use a different type of cable.

 If you wish to do so, you can have both ATA and SATA drives connected to your system.

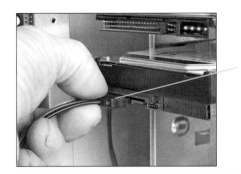

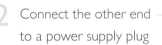

1 Connect one end of the power cable to the socket at the left of the drive

 To complete the installation, you will have to install the SATA driver when back in Windows. This will be on the motherboard's installation disk.

2 Connect the other end to a power supply plug

 If the SATA drive is intended to be the boot drive, and assuming the operating system is Windows XP, you will have to do the following:

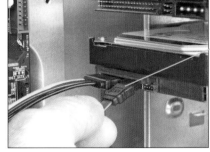

3 Connect one end of the interface cable to the socket at the right of the power supply socket

- Copy the SATA driver to a floppy disk
- Install the drive
- Start the XP installation
- When prompted, press F6 to install RAID or SCSI drivers
- When prompted for the driver, place the floppy disk in the drive, select the driver and press Enter

4 Connect the other end to the SATA1 socket on the motherboard. This is for the primary drive. The SATA2 socket is for a second SATA drive

RAID Configurations

Some motherboards provide an integrated RAID controller. If yours doesn't, you will have to either buy a RAID controller PCI card, or use a software RAID controller.

For those of you who have two or more hard drives in your system, there is another configuration option. This is known as RAID (Redundant Array of Independant Disks), and it is a method of configuring a combination of hard drives so as to gain specific benefits, such as data protection and increased performance.

This type of configuration is set up after the drives have been installed and requires either a hardware RAID controller, or a RAID software program (see middle margin note).

The various RAID configurations are:

RAID 0

This requires a minimum of two drives, and works by splitting the data equally between them (this is known as striping). The result is much improved data transfer speeds as each drive handles part of a file.

Software RAID controllers place a heavy load on the operating system, and thus have an adverse effect on overall system performance. Nor are they as reliable or efficient as hardware controllers.

RAID 1

This also requires a minimum of two drives. In this configuration, all data saved is duplicated (known as mirroring) on each drive. The purpose is data protection – if one drive fails, the data is recoverable from the other(s).

RAID 0+1

This is a combination of RAID 0 and RAID 1 and requires a minimum of four drives. Half the drives are used to stripe the data, and the other half to mirror it. Thus, it provides fast data transfer, together with data protection.

RAID setups are expensive and are most commonly found in server and corporate environments. Unless you have a need for extreme levels of performance or data protection, they really aren't necessary.

RAID 5

This requires a minimum of three drives. Data is striped across all the drives, but an error-checking bit (known as the parity bit), is also stored. Should any one drive fail, the RAID controller will calculate the missing data and keep the system running until the faulty drive can be replaced.

Partitioning and Formatting

Partitioning is the process of defining specific areas of a hard disk for use by the operating system.

An internal hard drive must be partitioned before it can be used. This procedure prepares the drive for use by the operating system (see margin note). If a drive is not partitioned, it won't be recognized by the system – if you go to My Computer, it won't be visible there.

Drives can be split into a number of partitions, each of which appears to the operating system as a separate hard drive. Alternatively, one partition equal to the entire capacity of the drive can be created – this is the usual setup.

When the partition has been created, it must then be formatted. This process organizes it into logical units known as blocks, sectors, and tracks. These are used by the operating system to "remember" where specific data is stored on the drive.

The procedure varies according to which version of Windows you are using and for those of you running Windows 95, 98 or Me, these are the systems we'll explain the procedure for first.

Users of Windows 95, 98 and Me will need a startup disk. This should have been supplied by the manufacturer. If not, make one as described on this page.

Before you start, you will need a startup disk, which enables the system to be booted. If you haven't got one, do the following:

1 Place a blank floppy disk in the floppy drive

2 Go to My Computer and right-click the floppy drive. Select Format

3 Select Copy system files and then click OK

4 When the format procedure has finished, the startup disk is ready for use

Partitioning and Formatting With Windows 95, 98 and Me

1 Place the startup disk in the floppy drive and restart the PC. It will now boot from the disk giving you access to the partitioning and formatting tools

```
Microsoft Windows 98 Startup Menu

1. Start computer with CD-ROM support.
2. Start computer without CD-ROM support.
3. View the Help file.

Enter a choice: 1        Time remaining: 21
```

2 Select option 1 and press Enter

```
This may take a few minutes. Please wait...

Windows 98 has detected that drive C does not contain a valid FAT or
FAT32 partition. There are several possible causes.

1.  The drive may need to be partitioned. To create a partition on the drive,
run FDISK from the MS-DOS command prompt.

2.  You may be using third-party disk-partitioning software. If you are using
this type of software, remove the Emergency Boot Disk and restart your
computer. Then, follow the on-screen instructions to start your computer from
a floppy disk.

3.  Some viruses also cause your drive C to not register. You can use a virus
scanning program to check your computer for viruses.

The diagnostic tools were successfully loaded to drive C.

MSCDEX Version 2.25
Copyright (C) Microsoft Corp. 1986-1995. All rights reserved.
        Drive D: = Driver MSCD001 unit 0

To get help, type HELP and press ENTER.

A:\>fdisk
```

3 At the A:\> prompt, type fdisk

```
Your computer has a disk larger than 512 MB. This version of Windows
includes improved support for large disks, resulting in more efficient
use of disk space on large drives, and allowing disks over 2 GB to be
formatted as a single drive.

IMPORTANT: If you enable large disk support and create any new drives on this
disk, you will not be able to access the new drive(s) using other operating
systems, including some versions of Windows 95 and Windows NT, as well as
earlier versions of Windows and MS-DOS. In addition, disk utilities that
were not designed explicitly for the FAT32 file system will not be able
to work with this disk. If you need to access this disk with other operating
systems or older disk utilities, do not enable large drive support.

Do you wish to enable large disk support (Y/N)...........? [Y]
```

4 Ignore this message. Type Y and then press Enter

5   Type 1 and press Enter (note that if you are installing a second hard drive, you will see a fifth option – "Change current fixed disk drive". Select this by typing 5 and then press Enter)

```
                      Microsoft Windows 98
                     Fixed Disk Setup Program
             (C)Copyright Microsoft Corp. 1983 - 1998

                          FDISK Options

Current fixed disk drive: 1

Choose one of the following:

1. Create DOS partition or Logical DOS Drive
2. Set active partition
3. Delete partition or Logical DOS Drive
4. Display partition information


Enter choice: [1]




Press Esc to exit FDISK
```

6   Type 1 and then press Enter

```
               Create DOS Partition or Logical DOS Drive

Current fixed disk drive: 1

Choose one of the following:

1. Create Primary DOS Partition
2. Create Extended DOS Partition
3. Create Logical DOS Drive(s) in the Extended DOS Partition




Enter choice: [1]




Press Esc to return to FDISK Options
```

7   Type Y and then press Enter to create the partition

```
                     Create Primary DOS Partition

Current fixed disk drive: 1

Do you wish to use the maximum available size for a Primary DOS Partition
and make the partition active (Y/N)....................? [Y]









Press Esc to return to FDISK Options
```

```
You MUST restart your system for your changes to take effect.
Any drives you have created or changed must be formatted
AFTER you restart.

Shut down Windows before restarting.



    Press Esc to exit FDISK_
```

8 Press Esc to exit fdisk and reboot. The PC will now return to the A:\> prompt

```
Preparing to start your computer.
This may take a few minutes. Please wait...

The diagnostic tools were successfully loaded to drive D.

MSCDEX Version 2.25
Copyright (C) Microsoft Corp. 1986-1995. All rights reserved.
        Drive E: = Driver MSCD001 unit 0

To get help, type HELP and press ENTER.

A:\>format c:

WARNING, ALL DATA ON NON-REMOVABLE DISK
DRIVE C: WILL BE LOST!
Proceed with Format (Y/N)?Y_
```

9 Type format c:

The drive will now be formatted

```
WARNING, ALL DATA ON NON-REMOVABLE DISK
DRIVE C: WILL BE LOST!
Proceed with Format (Y/N)?Y

Formatting 4,094.66M
Format complete.
Writing out file allocation table
Complete.
Calculating free space (this may take several minutes)...
Complete.

Volume label (11 characters, ENTER for none)?

4,285,165,568 bytes total disk space
4,285,165,568 bytes available on disk

    4,096 bytes in each allocation unit.
1,046,182 allocation units available on disk.

Volume Serial Number is 3315-130B

A:\>_
```

10 When prompted to enter a volume label just press Enter. Then exit fdisk, remove the startup disk and restart the PC. The drive will now be visible in My Computer

Installing Windows 95, 98 and Me

If the drive being installed is intended to be the boot drive (the one on which Windows is loaded), you will now have to install Windows on it.

This is simply a continuation of the partitioning and formatting procedure that we have just described.

If the drive being partitioned and formatted is the one on which the operating system will be loaded, this will now have to be installed.

Refer to Step 10 (page 86). Instead of removing the startup disk, leave it in the floppy drive. Restart the PC and repeat Step 2 (page 84)

```
Preparing to start your computer.
This may take a few minutes. Please wait...

The diagnostic tools were successfully loaded to drive D.

MSCDEX Version 2.25
Copyright (C) Microsoft Corp. 1986-1995. All rights reserved.
        Drive E: = Driver MSCD001 unit 0

To get help, type HELP and press ENTER.

A:\>d:setup
Please wait while Setup initializes.

Setup is now going to perform a routine check on your system.

To continue, press ENTER. To quit Setup, press ESC._
```

2 At the A:\> prompt, type d:setup and press Enter

The Windows installation routine will now begin. Simply follow the prompts to complete the installation.

Partitioning and Formatting With Windows XP

To partition and format a hard drive from within Windows, do the following:

- *In the Control Panel, open Administrative Tools. Click Computer Management and then Disk Management*

- *In the right-hand window, you will see a list of the drives installed in the system. Simply right-click the required drive to access the partitioning and formatting options*

A big advantage provided by Windows XP is that there is no need for a startup disk – the partitioning and formatting tools are on the installation disc.

However, there is a prerequisite. The system must be configured to boot from the CD-ROM drive. Do this as follows:

1 Restart the PC and enter the BIOS setup program as described previously

2 On the main page, select Advanced BIOS Features and press Enter

```
           Phoenix - AwardBIOS CMOS Setup Utility
                   Advanced BIOS Features

    Virus Warning                [Disabled]        Item Help
    CPU Internal Cache           [Enabled]
    External Cache               [Enabled]    Menu Level   ►
    CPU L2 Cache ECC Checking     [Enabled]
    Quick Power On Self Test     [Enabled]    Select Your Boot
    First Boot Device            [CDROM]      Device Priority.
    Second Boot Device           [HDD-0]
    Third Boot Device            [CDROM]
    Boot Other Device            [Enabled]
    Swap Floppy Drive            [Disabled]
    Boot Up Floppy Seek          [Enabled]
    Bootup NumLock Status        [On]
    Gate A20 Option              [Fast]
    Typematic Rate Setting       [Disabled]
  X Typematic Rate (Chars/Sec)   6
  X Typematic Delay (Msec)       250
    Security Option              [Setup]
    OS Select For Dram > 64MB    [Non-OS2]
    HDD S.M.A.R.T Capability     [Enabled]
```

To use XP's partitioning and formatting tools, the CD-ROM drive must be set as the first boot device. Otherwise, they won't be accessible.

3 Scroll down to First Boot Device, and using the Page Up/Page Down keys, select CDROM. Save the change and exit the BIOS

You should restore the boot order to its original setting when the partitioning and formatting procedure is complete. If you forget the original order, the first boot device should be the floppy drive, followed by the hard drive and CD-ROM drive respectively.

4 With the CD-ROM drive configured as the first boot device, insert the XP installation disc into the drive and boot the PC. When the second boot screen flashes up, look at the bottom and you'll see a message that says "Press any key to boot from CD...". Follow these instructions, and after a short period XP's installation routine will begin. Work through the first two screens, which will be "Welcome to Setup" and the license agreement. If you are using an upgrade disc, you will be asked for a full version of Windows after the license agreement. Otherwise, you will then see the installation options screen, as shown below

```
Windows XP Home Edition Setup

   The following list shows the existing partitions and
   unpartitioned space on this computer.

   Use the UP and DOWN ARROW keys to select an item in the list.

      •  To set up Windows XP on the selected item, press ENTER.

      •  To create a partition in the unpartitioned space, press C.

      •  To delete the selected partition, press D.

   4095 MB Disk 0 at Id 0 on bus 0 on atapi [MBR]
         Unpartitioned space                    44095 MB
```

5 In the box, you will see the total size of the drive next to "Unpartitioned space". If you press Enter, XP will create a single partition equal to this size

If you wish to create two or more partitions, press C and then follow the onscreen instructions

For the purpose of this tutorial, however, we will assume that you want a single partition, so just press Enter. The partition will then be created and you will then be taken to the format screen as shown on the next page

XP allows you to format the drive in one of two file systems, NTFS or FAT. Unless you are planning to make use of XP's multi-boot facility that allows two or more operating systems to be installed on the same PC, choose the NTFS option. Without going into the reasons, this will be the best choice.

You also have the option of doing a "Quick" format. Use this only if the drive is brand new, as this option does not check the disk for errors, such as bad sectors.

6 The format screen offers two options: the NTFS or FAT file systems. Choose the one you want and press Enter. The new partition will now be formatted with the chosen file system

```
Windows XP Home Edition Setup

A new partition for Windows XP has been created on
4095 MB Disk 0 at Id 0 on bus 0 on atapi [MBR].

This partition must now be formatted.

From the list below, select a file system for the new partition.
Use the UP and DOWN ARROW keys to select the file system you want,
and then press ENTER.

If you want to select a different partition for Windows XP,
press ESC.

    Format the partition using the NTFS file system (Quick)
    Format the partition using the FAT file system (Quick)
    Format the partition using the NTFS file system
    Format the partition using the FAT file system
```

Now all you have to do is sit back as the Windows XP installation routine automatically begins copying files to the hard drive.

```
Windows XP Home Edition Setup

                Please wait while Setup copies files
                to the Windows installation folders.
            This might take several minutes to complete.


    Setup is copying files...
                                    39%
    [                                        ]
```

Don't forget to restore the original boot order when you have finished.

Simply follow the prompts and within twenty minutes or so, the installation will be complete.

Note: The above procedure is necessary only if the drive is going to be used as the boot drive. If it is a second drive for additional storage purposes, it can be partitioned and formatted from within Windows.

Removable Media Drive Options

This chapter looks at drives that provide a more permanent, and thus reliable, means of data storage than offered by hard drives.

Of all the drives currently on the market, optical (CD/DVD) writers are the most popular, due mainly to the low cost of the media. One aspect of these devices that causes confusion is the variety of formats they use; we explain what these are and their pros and cons.

Also available are the drives that use magnetic media and operate more like a hard drive. We see how these compare with optical drives.

Covers

Chapter Six

Floppy Drives – Are they Worth it?

While these devices are painfully slow and the disks hold a pitiful amount of data by today's standards – only 1.44 MB – they are, nevertheless, still useful in many ways. Some typical applications are: small hardware drivers (mice, keyboards, etc), BIOS flash upgrades, rescue disks, and text documents (a floppy disk will hold a full-length novel).

The big advantage offered by the floppy drive is the fact that nearly every PC owner has one. Thus, they provide a near universal method of transporting data. This is not the case with the other types of removable media drives.

So a floppy drive that has failed is usually worth replacing, particularly as they cost only a few dollars.

Is it worth replacing a good one with a more recent model, though? Will there be any performance gains? The short answer to this is no, as the basic technology behind them hasn't changed for years. A drive bought today will be no faster than one bought five years ago.

However, some of today's floppy drives do come with an additional feature that will be useful to many users. This is a built-in flash card reader. Apart from handling floppy disks, these drives can also read, and transfer to the hard drive, the contents of various types of flash memory. For example: Compact Flash, MicroDrive, MemoryStick, SmartMedia, MultiMedia, and Secure Digital Cards.

With a suitably equipped floppy drive, you can look at the pictures on your digital camera directly from the memory card.

Also available is an advanced type of floppy drive known as a Superdisk drive. These devices have exactly the same dimensions as a standard floppy drive and are compatible with 1.44 MB floppy disks. However, they can also be used with a different type of disk, a superdisk, that has capacities of up to 250 MB. Furthermore, they incorporate a formatting technology that increases the capacity of a floppy disk to a comparatively massive 32 MB.

So if you have a need for any of these features, a floppy drive upgrade can be worthwhile.

Installing a Floppy Drive

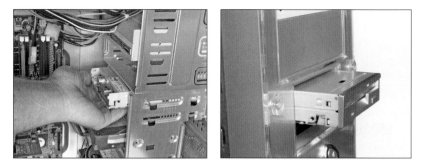

The floppy drive bay is at the top of the lower 3.5 inch drive cage.

Slide the drive into the top of the 3.5 inch drive cage (above the hard drive). You can do this from the rear or from the front

2 Secure the drive

Power is supplied to the floppy drive via the 4-pin connector, as shown below.

3 Connect the power supply

The red stripe corresponds to pin 1 on both the motherboard and the drive sockets.

Unlike those for hard drives, floppy drive interface connectors are not keyed at the drive end. This makes it possible to fit them the wrong way round. To make sure that you don't do this, the cable has a red stripe along one side and also a twist at one end, as shown left. The twisted end connects to the drive, with the stripe on the left-hand side, as shown below.

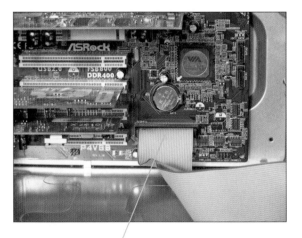

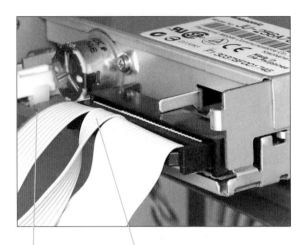

4 Red stripe on the left, twisted end to the drive

5 The motherboard connector is keyed, so it will only fit one way (red stripe on the left)

CD-ROM Drives

A CD-ROM drive can read the data on a CD but can do no more than that; it cannot write data. For this reason, these devices

are one of the most commonly upgraded parts of a PC, as writing capability is an essential function for many people these days. When considering a replacement, the upgrader has a number of options from which to choose:

Rotational speed is not nearly as important an issue as it is with hard drives. The performance differential between a 32x drive and a 58x drive is negligible.

1) Firstly, a like-for-like swap can be made, i.e. a CD-ROM drive for a CD-ROM drive. This is rather pointless though, as explained in option 2 below. About the only improvement that you will see is a marginal increase in data transfer rates due to the higher rotational speed of newer drives

CD writers can do everything that a CD-ROM drive can, and more. Furthermore, they cost the same.

2) The CD-ROM drive can be replaced with a CD writer. These devices cost exactly the same as a CD-ROM drive but are also able to write to CDs, as well as read from them. Given this fact, it would be crazy to stick with CD-ROM

3) The upgrader also has two DVD options. The first is a DVD-ROM drive, which, as with the CD-ROM drive, is only able to read discs. However, they are able to read CDs as well as DVDs. The second is a DVD writer, which as well as being able to read DVDs and CDs, can also write to a DVD disc (but not to a CD)

If all this sounds confusing, we're sorry to have to tell you that it gets worse. Discs for CD and DVD writers come in a variety of formats, all of which have their pros and cons. Furthermore, there are compatibility issues with these formats – some drives can read certain formats but not others.

Making sure that you get the correct type of drive and associated format to suit your needs requires a bit of homework. The following pages will help to guide you through the CD/DVD format maze.

CD Writers

When these drives were first introduced, the discs they used were only capable of being written to once (CD-R). It wasn't long, though, before re-writable models (CD-RW), which could erase the contents of a disc and reuse it, hit the market. These required a disc of a different composition that allowed rewriting.

CD rewriters (CD-RW) are now standard in new PCs, and more upmarket PCs may also include a DVD drive. The older CD writers (CD-R) have been phased out.

So when you come to upgrade your old CD-ROM drive, a CD-RW is probably the drive you will go for. Even if you presently have no need for disc writing, this is a feature that you will undoubtedly find a use for in the future. In the meantime, it will read your CDs.

You may, of course, already have a CD-R drive in your system and might be considering upgrading to a CD-RW. In this case, you need to know the pros and cons of the two types of disc.

CD-R

This is the most commonly used type of writable disc. They are cheap, the writing process is quicker than it is with CD-RW, and they have a longer expected shelf-life than CD-RWs. They are also considered to be more reliable, i.e. there is less chance of data corruption.

CD-R discs are the best choice for virtually all purposes. They are cheaper, quicker in operation and offer more reliable storage than CD-RW discs. Another advantage is that they are more compatible with home and car CD players.

CD-RW

The big advantage of these discs (indeed, the only advantage) is that they can be reused – if you believe what the manufacturers say – about a thousand times over.

So unless you do a lot of non-permanent disc writing, the advice is to stick with your CD-R drive.

DVD Drives

For those of you who may be interested, DVD's successor is already knocking at the door. Known as Blu-ray (after the color of the laser beam employed), the technology is essentially the same but offers storage capacities of 50 GB per disc (100 GB on dual-layer discs).

Blu-ray drives for PCs are expected to be available in the USA sometime in 2006. They will, however, be very expensive, as will the discs. The good news for the well-heeled upgrader is that Blu-ray drives will be backward compatible with CDs and DVDs

If you like to be at the cutting edge and can afford it, you may want to wait until this technology becomes available before upgrading your present drive.

DVD (Digital Versatile Disc) is an optical data technology that provides extremely high storage capacities. A standard DVD can hold 4.7 GB of data, and a dual-layer DVD (which has two data layers) can hold 8.5 GB.

For this reason, DVD discs are used for commercially produced movies, as an entire movie can be fitted on one disc. These seriously high levels of storage capacity are also beginning to be utilized by the PC industry. For example, Microsoft's Encarta Reference Library, which requires five CDs, is available on a single DVD. With the ever increasing size of software applications, you can expect to see many more of them shipped on DVD discs in the near future. This is one reason to buy a DVD drive.

Another advantage of DVD writers is that they write data faster than CD writers do. See page 99 for more on this.

The high capacity of DVD discs is handy for PC users as well. Typical applications are large-scale system backups, and storage of high-resolution video and TV shows recorded via TV tuner devices. Another plus for these drives is the fact that they can also read CDs (both software CDs and writable CDs). This makes them the most versatile type of optical drive presently available.

The upgrader thinking of buying a DVD drive will find that they are available in three versions: read-only, writable, and rewritable. The reasons for choosing between these are the same as those for choosing between the various sorts of CD drive.

The issue of DVD formats also needs to be considered. Currently, there are three of these.

DVD–. Introduced in 1999, this format is supported by Panasonic, Toshiba, Apple, Hitachi, NEC, Pioneer, Samsung, and Sharp. It is available in write-once versions (DVD–R) and rewrite versions (DVD–RW).

If your primary purpose for buying a DVD drive is long-term data storage, consider one of the DVD-RAM drives. DVD-RAM discs are commonly housed in a protective caddy, similar to those of floppy and Zip disks. They have the highest life expectancy of all the formats. Furthermore, the drives themselves provide data protection facilities, e.g. the marking of bad sectors. These features make DVD-RAM the most reliable format.

DVD+. This is a more recent format that was introduced in 2002, and is supported by Philips, Sony, Hewlett-Packard, Dell, Ricoh, Yamaha, and others. As with DVD–, write-once (DVD+R) and rewrite (DVD+RW) versions are available.

DVD-RAM. A DVD-RAM disc is very similar to a hard drive in that files can be dragged and dropped. This format also offers faster data access and higher levels of reliability than the + and – formats. However, DVD-RAM discs can be read only in a DVD-RAM drive – the format is not compatible with DVD+ and DVD– drives.

Summary

The DVD+ format is more advanced than DVD–. It offers faster write speeds, slightly higher disc capacity, and in-built data correction. However, DVD+ discs are more expensive than DVD– and the format is generally considered to be less compatible with home and car DVD players.

So which one do you go for? For general-purpose use, the choice is between DVD+ and DVD–. While there are technical differences (see margin note) between them, to all intents and purposes, they can be considered to be the same. So either will be fine. In any case, most current DVD writers are compatible with both formats.

Users who write data frequently, and access written data, will be best served by the hard drive-like qualities of the DVD-RAM format. This format is also the best one for long-term data storage purposes due to its reliability. Remember that it does have compatibility issues with other formats, though.

Before You Buy a CD/DVD Drive

Having decided what type of drive you want, the next thing is to take a closer look at these devices and see what they actually offer. The following are the factors you need to consider:

Interface

The interface used by the drive is something that you don't need to worry about unless you are looking to "future-proof" your system. The ATA interface, which is used by most drives, is quite capable of running the drives currently on the market at their full potential.

The vast majority of drives currently on the market use the ATA interface (with an extension known as ATAPI). They are also available with USB, FireWire, SCSI and SATA interfaces, which all offer *potentially* faster data transfer rates (see margin note).

Read/Write Speeds

The speed at which a drive reads and writes is indicated by "x" ratings in the specifications. Usually, these are also marked prominently on the packaging, as shown below. Using this as a typical example, the first figure, 40x, is the speed at which the

drive writes to a CD-R. The second, 12x, is the speed at which it writes to a CD-RW, and the third figure, 48x, is its read speed.

However, for these figures to have any meaning, you need to know what the x represents. In the case of CD drives, it represents 150 KB/s. So the CD drive in our example above has a CD-R write speed of 6.0 MB/s (150 KB/s x 40).

The lower x ratings of DVD drives do not mean that these drives are slower than CD drives. They read data just as quickly and actually write data more quickly.

DVD drives also use this convention. You will notice though, that the x ratings are much lower, typically 16x, 4x, 16x. On the face of it, this would seem to indicate that DVD drives are slower than CD drives. However, they are actually much faster, and this is because the x represents 1.32 MB/s (as opposed to 150 KB/s with CD drives). So a 16x rating indicates a write speed of 21 MB/s.

Specifications

Specs to look out for include:

Writing Mode. A very important factor in the performance of an optical drive is the maintenance of a constant data transfer rate across the entire disc. To achieve this, manufacturers use one of three methods: Constant Linear Velocity (CLV), Zoned Constant Linear Velocity (ZCLV) and Constant Angular Velocity (CAV). All you need to know here is that budget and mid-range drives use the CLV or ZCLV method, while top-end models use CAV.

Access Time. This is the time needed to locate a specific item of data on the disc. This metric is measured in milliseconds and you should look for a figure no higher than 100 ms.

Buffer Size. Optical drives use a buffer to ensure that data flows to the disc smoothly and without interruption during the writing process; this helps to eliminate errors. Typically, drives are supplied with a 2 MB buffer and this is the minimum that you should accept. High-quality drives have buffers as large as 8 MB.

Recommended Media

If you already have a collection of written discs, it is worth making sure that the drive you are going to buy will be able to play them.

The build quality of CDs and DVDs varies widely and some drives have trouble with low-quality discs. To enable users to avoid this potential problem, most manufacturers provide a list of media recommended for use with their drives, as in this example:

Recommended Media		(All DVD-RW and CD-RW media is rewritable up to 1,000 times)
DVD+R	16X	Taiyo Yuden, Verbatim/Mitsubishi
	8X, 4X	Maxell, Ricoh, Taiyo Yuden, Verbatim/Mitsubishi
DVD+RW	4X	Ricoh, Verbatim/Mitsubishi
DVD+R DL	8X, 4X	Verbatim/Mitsubishi
DVD-R	16X, 8X, 4X	Maxell, Taiyo Yuden, TDK, Verbatim/Mitsubishi
DVD-RW	4X, 2X	TDK, Verbatim/Mitsubishi
DVD-R DL	4X	Verbatim/Mitsubishi, Victor
CD-R	48X	Maxell, Taiyo Yuden, TDK
	40X	Ricoh
CD-RW	32X, 24X	Verbatim/Mitsubishi
	10X, 4X	Ricoh, Verbatim/Mitsubishi Chemical

Dual-Layer Technology

If you are tempted by the high storage capacities offered by dual-layer DVDs, remember that they will be an expensive way of saving your data.

This is the latest DVD innovation and it doubles the maximum storage capacity of a DVD to 8.5 GB. However, dual-layer discs can only be written and read by a dual-layer drive. Also, 8.5 GB dual-layer discs currently cost three times as much as a single-layer 4.7 GB disc, which makes them poor value for money.

Installing a CD/DVD Drive

I Slide the drive into the drive bay from the front (if you try doing it from the back, the PSU will block access)

2 Screw the drive in place

With some drives an audio cable is not necessary as they use the interface cable to make the connection to the sound system. These drives use a technology called Digital Audio Extraction (DAE).

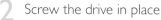

3 If your drive has an audio cable to connect it to the sound system, plug one end into the socket at the far left

80-pin interface cables are keyed to make sure they fit correctly. However, the older 40-pin cables are not, so it is possible to fit these the wrong way. If this is what you are using, keep the striped edge on the right-hand side.

4 Keeping the striped edge on the right-hand side, plug the interface cable into the drive

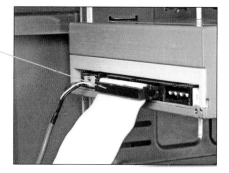

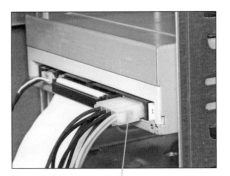

5 Hook up the power supply

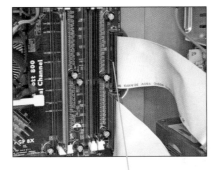

6 Connect the drive to the black
socket on the motherboard

7 Connect the audio cable to
the sound system

If you are installing a second drive, perhaps a DVD drive, the first step is to set it as the slave, as shown below. Then at step 4 (on the previous page), plug the slave connector (as shown on page 80, step 3) into the drive. Otherwise, the procedure is exactly the same.

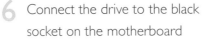

Then reboot and you will see your new drive listed next to either Secondary Master or Secondary Slave.

Other Types of Drive

The upgrader looking to add extra storage options to the system has three choices, apart from optical drive writers.

Zip drives are the perfect solution for people who need a quick and flexible means of storing small amounts of data.

Zip/Rev Drives

The first two options are the Zip and Rev drives from Iomega. These are basically a souped-up version of the floppy disk drive and work in much the same way. The differences lie in the speed at which they operate, the level of storage capacity offered, and the range of features and options provided.

Zip drive   Rev Drive

Iomega used to produce a Jaz drive as well. While this product has been discontinued, it is still available from many retailers. Should you consider buying one, be aware that media manufacturers are no longer making the disks.

These drives offer some real advantages over the CD/DVD method of data storage and transfer.

● Unlike writable disc drives, they do not need an associated software program

● They work just like a hard drive. This means you can save to them from a program's Save As file menu command and by drag and drop. Also, data can rearranged on the disks

● Data transfer speeds are much higher

A very useful feature offered by Zip and Rev drives is password protection.

● The disks are housed in a tough plastic case, which makes them less susceptible to physical damage

● They provide a range of features, such as password protection and integrated backup facilities

● Rev drive disks provide higher storage capacity

Disks for Zip drives are available in capacities of 100, 250 and 750 MB. Rev disks provide a massive 35 GB of storage.

Media for Zip and Rev drives are extremely expensive on a dollar/capacity ratio compared to other types of storage media.

The Rev drive is designed for users who have large-scale backup requirements. In operation, it has data transfer speeds similar to a hard drive, and thus provides one of the best backup solutions currently on the market.

The only drawback with these drives is the cost of the media: a single 250 MB Zip disk costs approximately $10, while a single Rev disk costs some $55. If you buy them in packs, though, the cost does come down.

Tape Drives

Tape drives intended for use in a PC are very similar in appearance to a CD or DVD drive. The media they use, as you might expect, is tape and comes in the form of a cassette, much like the old music cassettes that were around years ago.

Typically, these devices are used in corporate environments where massive data backups are carried out on a regular basis. However, users who run a business from home might consider one of these drives (assuming they are prepared to spend the minimum of $600 that they cost).

The tape cassette or cartridge can typically hold 20 GB of data, although compression techniques can increase this to a maximum of 40 GB. The drives have a data transfer rate of around 5 MB/s, which means that a 20 GB cartridge will be filled to capacity in about an hour.

The big advantage of tape drives (once you've recovered from the shock of parting with $600, or more, for one) is that the cartridges themselves are cheap – $10 for a 20 GB tape – and can be reused any number of times.

See and Hear More With Your PC

In this chapter, we consider the options available to upgraders who want to improve the audio and video capabilities of their PCs.

In both cases, the upgrader can go for either an integrated solution or a stand-alone device. We look at the merits of both.

Video is probably the most popular leisure activity of all, and a suitably equipped PC can provide the video enthusiast with a range of options that are not available from a collection of stand-alone devices. To find out what these are and what's required in terms of hardware, read on.

We also look at speaker systems – types, applications and important specifications.

Covers

Chapter Seven

Computer Video Systems

Video systems for computers come in two types: integrated video (built in to the motherboard), and video cards. Both have pros and cons that make them suitable for some purposes and unsuitable for others. It is essential to know what these are in order to get the one most appropriate for your requirements.

Integrated Video Systems

For routine, every-day tasks, such as word processing and email, integrated video systems are more than adequate. Recent systems will even play 3D games to a fairly high standard.

Integrated video is a feature found on the majority of mainstream motherboards (although it is not always used). It is usually incorporated into the chipset and provides a low-cost video option for both users and manufacturers.

Until fairly recently, however, the quality of video produced by these systems has not been good. On older PCs, it may not even provide 3D, which is essential for many PC games and certain other types of application. However, more recent systems do provide a quality of video that is good enough for all but the most demanding applications.

The issue of system degradation needs to be put into context. For most people, the performance hit made by integrated systems is negligible and, in fact, will probably not even be noticed. On the other hand, users of poorly specified computers trying to run today's video-intensive applications will almost certainly notice it.

Another problem is caused by the demands made by integrated video on the computer's resources. Video processing needs a powerful processor and a good supply of RAM, and integrated video doesn't have either. Thus, the computer's CPU and RAM have to be used, with the result that other parts of the system may be short-changed in terms of CPU and RAM resources. Overall, system performance is adversely affected.

Reasons to Upgrade

There aren't any. If your PC is no more than two to three years old, your existing integrated system should be capable of handling whatever you throw at it with the possible exception of 3D games, and heavy-duty applications.

Upgrading an integrated video system to a better one will mean buying a new motherboard.

Older computers may well benefit. But as the upgrade is going to involve a motherboard replacement, which turns the job into a major upgrade, a much simpler option would just be to add a video card. Even a low-end model that will probably cost less than a new motherboard will provide you with all the video processing capabilities required.

Video Cards

Video cards provide a much higher level of video quality as they are designed specifically for this purpose. To this end, they come equipped with their own processor and memory, which means that the system's CPU and memory are free to carry out other unrelated functions. This results in faster overall system performance.

Video in all its various forms – commercial movies, TV, home movies and so on – is one of the most popular applications in home computing these days. A high-quality video card provides users with many more options than an integrated system does.

A bonus is the fact that many video cards have integrated functions, which can help to justify the often high cost of these devices. A hardware DVD decoder is a typical example: this will play DVD movies much better than a software decoder would.

Bundled software, usually a couple of recent PC games, is often also included in the package.

By providing extra input/output sockets, video cards increase the range of video-related tasks that the PC can do. Importing video from external devices such as a VHS recorder is one example.

The big disadvantage of video cards is the cost. Top-end models that provide the latest technology are almost prohibitive in price. Even mid-range models will make a serious dent in your wallet.

There are also issues regarding the heat these devices produce, the noise they make, and the amount of space they occupy.

Reasons to Upgrade

There are four reasons to upgrade a video card, or to change from integrated video to a video card:

1) The existing card has failed

2) You start using an application that demands a high level of video-processing

3) You want to keep abreast of current video technology, such as the PCI Express interface

4) You need input/output sockets not provided by your existing system

Unravelling the Video Card Market

Browse through the video card section of a computer parts retailer or website and you will see models from a large number of manufacturers. What most people don't realize is that many of these cards are almost identical in terms of performance. This is because all these manufacturers use chips from one of two companies – ATI (the Radeon) and Nvidia (the Geforce) – which are very similar. (It's the same situation as with CPUs from Intel and AMD.)

In most cases, the chip used is detailed in the product name, e.g. the Chaintech GeForce FX 5500. Here, the manufacturer is Chaintech, the video chip is the Geforce, and the chip version is FX5500.

Because the chip basically defines the quality of the card, it follows that cards from different manufacturers that use the same chip will have similar levels of performance. So while it may seem that you have a large choice, many of the cards on offer are actually much the same.

Where they do differ is in the quality of the control circuitry and the specifications of associated components. For example, you can buy a card built around the ATI Radeon 9800 and featuring 256 MB of memory from one manufacturer, while another is offering a card with the same chip but with only 128 MB of memory.

Both the Radeon and Geforce chips are available in many versions, some of which are more highly specified than others. This allows the manufacturers to produce low-end, mid-range, and high-end video cards.

Regardless of these differences, however, the quality of the cards' output is going to be broadly similar because everything is driven, and controlled, by the chip.

So when differentiating between cards that use the same chip, you need to look at the "extras" provided by each card. These include integrated functions, the number and type of input/output sockets, dual-screen support, the amount and type of memory, etc. Don't forget the bundled software, either.

Video Card Specifications

There are so many video card specifications that it would be a herculean task to investigate them all. The following are the main ones and will give you a very good idea of a card's capabilities.

Memory

A good indicator of a video card's capabilities is the type of memory it uses. Top-end cards use DDR2 and DDR3.

An ample amount of memory is crucial to good video performance. To this end, all video cards have their own memory chips, and the higher the capacity, the higher a card's potential performance. Note the word "potential". A large amount of memory will result in improved performance only if the application in question actually needs it. So don't buy an expensive 256 MB card unless you have an application that can use it.

A more important consideration is the type of memory used. Top-end cards use the super-fast DDR2 and DDR3. Budget and mid-range cards use the slower DDR.

RAMDAC

When looking at video card specs, you will notice that some of them have two Ramdacs. These cards provide support for two monitors.

The Random Access Memory Digital-to-Analog Converter is a chip that converts the digital signal received from the graphics processing unit (GPU) to an analog signal that is compatible with the monitor. The faster it does this, the better the card's performance. Look for a figure of at least 300 MHz. Good video cards will have a RAMDAC rated at 400 MHz.

Fill Rate

The fill rate indicates the speed at which the card can render a scene. It is a very useful indicator of a video card's capabilities and top-end cards will have a fill rate of ten billion pixels per second. Low-end cards will come in at around one billion pixels per second.

Vertices/Triangles

Nvidia use the term "vertices" and ATI use "triangles". Both refer to the hundreds, or even thousands, of triangular shaped objects that are used to construct a curved 3D image (the more of these there are, the more sharply defined the curve).

A top-end card uses 700–800 million triangles, while a low-end card uses about 60 million.

Important Factors to Consider

Input/Output Ports

Quite apart from the quality of video they produce, video cards also increase the user's options by allowing external video devices to be connected to the PC via its ports.

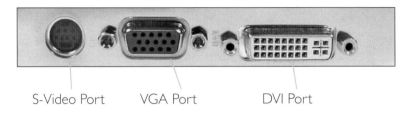

S-Video Port   VGA Port   DVI Port

Many video cards these days provide either two VGA or two DVI ports (and some provide one of each). The purpose is to allow the user to run two monitors from the same system. This can be useful for those who need plenty of desktop real estate.

The VGA (used to connect the monitor) and S-Video (used to connect external devices) ports are standard with virtually all cards.

There are many cards around, though, that do not provide a DVI (Digital Video Interface) output. Users of LCD monitors (which are digital devices), or those planning to buy one, should get a card with one of these as they provide a high quality digital signal.

Note that while it is possible to run an LCD monitor from the VGA port, the analog VGA signal then has to be converted to a digital one, and the conversion process does result in a slight reduction in picture quality.

DirectX

DirectX is a program interface designed to allow programmers to write applications without knowing exactly what hardware will be used to run them. Without going into the details, it provides a way of making an application compatible with as many different types of computer setup as possible.

If you play PC games, most of which require DirectX, you should make sure that the video card supports the latest version.

Most multimedia applications (3D games in particular), and applications containing an element of multimedia, are written around a specific version of DirectX and require it to be installed on the PC to function properly.

It is important that the video card supports the version of DirectX used by your applications, and the easiest way to ensure that it does is to buy one that supports the latest version.

Those of you who are looking to upgrade an AGP video card, or to upgrade from another video system to an AGP card, should be aware that this interface comes in various speeds – 1x, 2x, 4x, and 8x (currently, the fastest).

The AGP speed offered by the card must be supported by the motherboard. If it is higher, the card will still work but only at the maximum speed supported by the motherboard.

Interface

Most video cards currently use the AGP (Advanced Graphics Port) socket on the motherboard to connect to the system. This is a high-speed data bus designed specifically to handle the huge amounts of data associated with video.

However, AGP is now being phased out in favor of the newer PCI Express interface, which has a data transfer rate double that of AGP. Many video cards now coming on to the market use this new interface. The potential problem for upgraders is that PCI Express requires a PCI Express compatible motherboard (not to mention the bother of installing it). So unless you really do need the ultimate in video performance, it may be as well to wait until you can justify a motherboard upgrade. Then will be the time to go for PCI Express.

Power Requirements

This will be an issue only if you are considering one of the top-end cards. These devices use a lot of power and it may be that your PC's power supply unit (PSU) is simply not up to the job. If it isn't, it may blow and probably take your CPU and RAM with it.

Some of these cards require a 450 watt PSU but most PCs are only fitted with 300–400 watt PSUs. All the manufacturers advise what PSU their cards require in the specifications. Be sure to check this out because you may need to upgrade this device as well.

Another factor that may need to be considered when buying a top-end video card is its physical dimensions. These cards come with massive cooling systems that can block access to the nearest PCI socket. If all yours are in use, you may have to remove one of the devices from your system to make room for the video card. This is something that should be checked out in the card's specifications.

Heat

High-end video cards generate a lot of heat and PCs do not like it. Excess amounts can result in components failing long before they should and are also a major cause of system instability. While the cards themselves are adequately cooled by fans and heatsinks, these merely shift the heat to other parts of the system case and can cause other components to overheat.

Therefore, along with your new card, you may also need to install an extra fan or two (most cases have mounting points for these).

Installing a Video Card

Before you install a new video card, you are well advised to uninstall the driver for the old one, particularly if you are switching from ATI to Nvidia, or vice versa. This will prevent possible initial configuration problems.

Locate the colored AGP slot. This is above the white PCI slots

High-end video cards are heavy and bulky devices due to the massive cooling systems that they use. To prevent them slipping out of the slot, many motherboards these days supply a retaining clip.

2 Open the retaining clip (see margin note)

3 Fit the board into the socket. When it is fully inserted, the retaining clip will close automatically

When you've fitted the new card, its driver will need installing from the installation disk. Then go to Display in the Control Panel and set up the card according to your requirements.

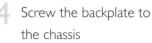

4 Screw the backplate to the chassis

Video Capture Devices

Video, with all its various activities (viewing, recording, editing, etc) is currently one of the most popular applications with PC users. One of the first questions people new to this ask is "How do I get the video into my PC"?

The answer is with the aid of a video capture card. There are several types of these and each has its pros and cons. The following will help you to decide which one is best for your purposes.

TV Tuners

As the name might suggest, these devices are concerned primarily with allowing you to watch television on your PC, either full-screen or in a resizable window.

Anyone buying a TV tuner with the intention of watching a lot of TV on the PC should choose a model that includes a remote control. Otherwise, you will have to get up and use the mouse or keyboard every time you want to switch channels or adjust the volume.

Low-end TV tuners are well known for locking up PCs. If you do not want to be constantly rebooting your computer, avoid the temptation to save a few dollars.

Available as either PCI cards or external models, they can display video from a variety of sources. These include standard TV antennas, cable networks, DVD players, camcorders and video recorders.

These devices can also be used to record TV (using the PC's hard drive as the recording medium), and to capture video from other types of video device.

The big advantage of TV tuners is that they provide two functions at a low cost: a) TV, and b) video capture facilities.

TV tuners do have their limitations, however. Very few of them provide a TV-out facility, which other types of capture card do. Also, recording formats offered can be limited: often only MPEG-2, which does not provide high-quality video.

That said, if your requirements in terms of video quality and features are not particularly high, these devices are adequate. For watching TV, they are fine. If you intend to do a lot of video work, though, or require high-quality output, a specialized video capture card will be a better option.

Video Cards

Most video cards provide video capturing facilities. Some, like the ATI All-In-Wonder, also come with an integrated TV tuner. As with TV tuners, though, video cards are designed with one specific purpose in mind; anything else they offer is of lesser importance, and thus may also be of lesser quality.

Associated sound can be an issue when using a video card to import video. Many of them do not have native support for sound and rely on the PC's sound system to do the job. With this type of setup, getting the sound to synchronize with the video can be problematic.

Another problem is that with the current need to provide both VGA and DVI outputs, video cards simply do not have enough room on the back plate to accommodate the full range of sockets necessary to connect all the various types of video device. In most cases a video in/video out (S-Video) socket is all you will get.

Video Capture Cards

For those who are serious about working with video, a dedicated capture card is by far the best option. These devices are also available as external models (shown below) that connect to the system via a USB or FireWire port.

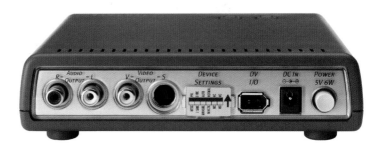

1394 sockets provide a high-speed FireWire connection for digital camcorders. This is a very useful option (if you use a camcorder) that is lacking in most home computer systems.

Apart from the higher level of overall quality provided, you will also get much more in the way of connectivity options, such as Mic, Line out, Composite Video Input, S-Video Input, and 4- and 6-pin 1394 (FireWire) sockets.

Other advantages include:

● A higher range of input and output formats
● Faster data transfer rates
● Higher capture resolutions and color depth capabilities
● The ability to export video as well as import it

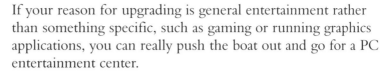

PC Entertainment Centers

If your reason for upgrading is general entertainment rather than something specific, such as gaming or running graphics applications, you can really push the boat out and go for a PC entertainment center.

These come in two types: a) a purpose-built unit, and b) a collection of home entertainment devices connected to, and controlled by, a PC. Both provide the following:

- TV
- DVD video
- CD audio
- Digital video recording (using the hard drive as the medium)
- Standard PC functions

The advantage of a purpose-built unit is that with the exception of the speakers and the TV, everything (the PC and the DVD and CD players) is housed in one compact unit. Not only is this a real space-saver; aesthetically, it looks much better – PCs are not the most attractive things to have in your living room.

These units do have several drawbacks, though. Firstly, buying one of these is more than a simple upgrade – they are not cheap. Secondly, being, essentially, a PC that requires cooling, and hence a fan, they make more noise than might be acceptable in a communal room. Thirdly, for close-up PC operations, such as word processing or using the Internet, the low resolution of a standard CRT TV will be inadequate. This means also buying a high-definition LCD monitor: a wide-screen model, assuming you watch DVD movies – and who doesn't, these days?

Building one yourself is a much cheaper option as you already have the PC and probably the other devices as well. All you need is a video capture device with the necessary inputs/outputs and you're in business.

The disadvantage is that the PC will usually have to be moved into the living room so that your TV, music system and CD/DVD players can be connected to it.

Computer Sound Systems

Integrated Sound

Virtually all motherboards provide an in-built sound system and the ones supplied with motherboards built in the last two or three years or so are actually very good, offering features such as support for multiple-speaker setups, DirectX, EAX and DirectSound 3D.

As with video, integrated sound systems do have a slightly adverse effect on system performance. Those of you upgrading with the intention of increasing the speed of the PC should be aware of this.

However, they do have three inherent disadvantages.

1) They are prone to picking up electrical interference from other motherboard components. This results in a low signal-to-noise ratio, which manifests itself as pops, clicks and buzzes in the output signal

2) Due to space restrictions on the motherboard's input/output panel, they do not provide the full range of sockets

3) Integrated systems do make a hit on overall system performance as they rely on the CPU to do all the number-crunching. While the effects are negligible, they are, nevertheless, there

Accordingly, integrated systems are not suitable for the following applications:

- High-quality sound reproduction
- Music mastering
- Hardcore gaming

The main sound requirement for gamers is 3D surround-sound, which requires 3D, and speaker connection, support. While current integrated systems provide both of these, the quality of 3D sound they offer is not as realistic as that offered by dedicated sound cards. The bottom line here is that if you want the best quality surround-sound, you will need a sound card. Otherwise, a recent integrated system will be adequate.

Users with an interest in any of these will need to install a separate sound card. A possible exception is gaming, depending on the degree of sophistication required (see margin note).

However, for all other purposes, an integrated sound system will be perfectly adequate.

With regard to upgrading an old integrated system to a more recent one that offers better quality and more features, this really doesn't make any sense as it will mean replacing the motherboard. A much easier, and probably cheaper, option would simply be to install a sound card. A mid-range, or maybe even a budget model, should do nicely.

Sound Cards

Sound cards are available with a range of specialized features and options, and if you're not careful, you could end up buying one that is not ideal for the task in hand.

Games and DVD Movies

For those of you who are seeking to enhance your game-playing or DVD movie experience in terms of sound, the quality of a sound card's output is of less importance than its ability to create the illusion that you are in the middle of the action literally. For example, if a game character walks behind you, you should hear footsteps that sound as though they are coming from over your shoulder.

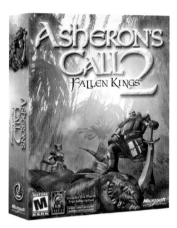

To be able to do this, the sound card must provide the following:

- Multiple-speaker support. Each pair of speakers requires a line-out socket. So a five- or six-speaker system will require three of these, and a seven- or eight-speaker system will require four

- 3D sound. Also known as Positional Audio, this technology accurately recreates the relative positioning of sound in a three-dimensional environment. The de facto standard is currently Creative's EAX. Also popular is Sensuara's 3DPA

 The term "channels" is also used to describe the number of speakers that can be connected to a sound card. For example, a three-channel card can support six speakers: two for each channel.

For gamers, DirectX is important and the card should support the version used by the games. Also important is the number of simultaneous sounds the card can process (these are referred to as channels in the specifications). If the application throws more of these at the sound card than it is designed to handle, the system's CPU has to help out, which makes a hit on overall system performance. The game's frame rate may also be adversely affected.

32 channels is a reasonable starting point; anything higher is good.

Music Systems

With the addition of a high-quality sound card and speakers, a PC can be turned into an audio system every bit as good as a

purpose-built unit. Furthermore, it will offer many more options, such as editing, disc writing, and storage facilities.

Although it may be desirable in such a system, 3D sound will be less important than the fidelity (purity) of the sound card's output. This is determined by the following specifications:

The most important specifications are bit-depth, which relates to the amount of data reproduced, and the signal-to-noise ratio, which relates to the amount of background noise (hiss).

- Bit-Depth. This describes how much of the original sound file is reproduced by the card. High bit-depth means high fidelity and dynamic range. CDs use a bit-depth of 16, so if your music collection is stored on this type of media, you need a 16-bit sound card. DVDs use a bit-depth of 24

- Sampling Rate. This determines the range of frequencies that can be converted to digital format by the sound card, and thus the accuracy of the reproduction. A good card will offer a sampling rate of at least 48 KHz

- Signal-to-Noise Ratio. This is a measure of how "clean" a sound signal is. The higher the amount of background noise (electrical interference, etc), the lower the signal-to-noise ratio (SNR). Low-end sound cards will have a SNR of some 75 decibels, while top-end cards will offer 100 decibels

- Total Harmonic Distortion. This is a measurement of the noise produced by the sound card itself during the process of converting the analog signal to a digital signal. A good quality card will have a THD of no more than 0.01%

Sound cards that come with a break-out box provide higher signal-to-noise ratios than those that don't. This is important for those who require as clean a signal as possible.

One problem inherent in all computers that can spoil an otherwise high-quality sound signal is electrical interference from other components. There are two ways to minimize this:

1) Isolate the sound card as far as possible (see page 120)

2) Buy a sound card that comes with a break-out box as shown below

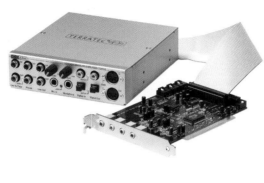

This unit either fits into a spare drive bay or sits on the desktop. It eliminates electrical interference by converting the analog signal to digital form before it is sent to the card in the PC.

Music Creation

Sound cards for musicians are the most complex of all. Not only must they provide a high-quality signal, they must also offer music mastering features, such as preamplifiers, synthesizers and wave-mixers.

S/PDIF connections are used for transferring digital data, and are found on most consumer video equipment. A sound card that includes this connection will ensure that users are able to hook up their PCs to these devices.

These cards almost always come with a break-out box as described above. Not only does this eliminate the issue of noise, the box also provides the full range of input/output sockets. These include balanced analog inputs/outputs, digital inputs/outputs in S/PDIF, ADAT, FireWire and MIDI, and a Phono (stereo) input. These cover virtually all types of device.

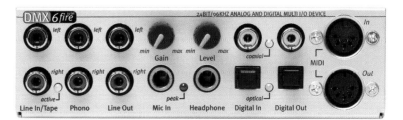

Installing a Sound Card

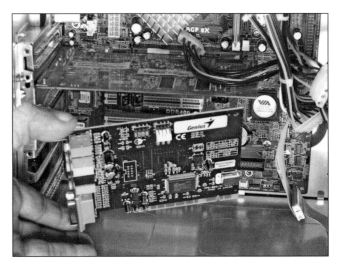

Maneuver the card into position

HOT TIP

On previous pages we have mentioned that sound cards are prone to picking up electrical interference from other system components. For this reason, you should install the card in the slot furthest from the other cards, i.e. right at the bottom, as shown opposite.

2 Slide the card into the PCI slot and press it home

3 Screw the backplate to the chassis

Speaker Systems

Surround-sound speaker systems range from 2:1 (one large subwoofer for bass reproduction, and two smaller satellites – one for mid-range and one for treble reproduction) up to 8:1 (one sub-woofer and seven satellites).

A good set of speakers is an essential part of a high-quality sound system. You may have the best sound card in the galaxy but if it is connected to a cheap speaker system, you will get poor sound.

PC speakers are available either as a pair (as supplied by most PC manufacturers) or as a multiple-speaker system. The type of setup you go for depends on the intended use.

Music buffs who simply want high fidelity will be best served by a pair of high-quality stereo speakers – a surround-sound system is not necessary.

Gamers and DVD movie fans who want surround-sound will need a multiple-speaker system, as shown below. When buying one of these, don't forget to check that your sound system is capable of fully utilizing it. There's no point in buying a 7:1 speaker system if you have only three line-out jacks.

20 Hz to 20 KHz is the range of frequencies that are audible to humans.

Whichever type of setup you go for, considering the following specifications will ensure that your chosen speakers are up to scratch.

- Frequency Response. This is the range of frequencies that the speakers can reproduce. The closer it is to the 20 Hz (bass) and 20 KHz (treble) thresholds, the better the output quality (see middle margin note)

Speaker wattage is rated in two ways: peak power and continuous power. The manufacturers like to emphasize the former as this is the higher of the two figures. However, buyers should be more concerned with the continuous (RMS) power rating as this gives a more accurate indication of the speaker's capabilities.

- Sensitivity. This is sometimes referred to as Sound Pressure Level and indicates the efficiency with which the speakers convert power to sound. Look for a figure of at least 90 decibels

- Wattage. While this is not an indication of quality, it is a fact that speakers with a high wattage rating do generally produce better sound

Speaker Installation

Installing PC speakers is simply a matter of plugging them into the sound system's output jacks. To make sure you get this right, most current sound cards and speakers use color-coded connections.

Front speakers plug into the green, rear speakers into the black, and center and side speakers into the orange sockets

Positioning Speakers

To get the best effect out of surround-sound systems, the speakers must be optimally placed. While there is a large degree of personal preference involved here, the following illustration of a 7:1 speaker system setup is a good guideline.

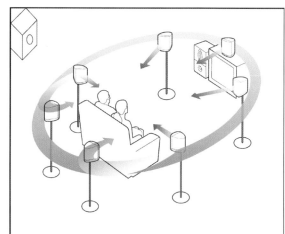

Firstly, the sub-woofer: this is not critical as bass is non-directional. However, the best results will be obtained from placing it next to a wall or in a corner.

The center speaker should be placed on top of the monitor or TV, and the front-right and -left speakers to either side and angled towards the listener.

Two speakers should be placed on either side and the final two at the rear.

Create a Reliable PC

For most people, an unreliable PC is no more than just a nuisance; they can live with the occasional crash and loss of non-essential data. For others, it can cause real problems and may even render the computer unfit for the purpose it was bought for.

This chapter focuses on the causes of an unreliable system and the upgrades that can be made in order to resolve these issues.

Covers

Chapter Eight

What Makes a PC Unreliable?

An unreliable PC is one that behaves erratically, does things that it shouldn't do, and doesn't do things that it should. Typical symptoms are frequent crashing, locking-up and sudden system reboots, all of which are common causes of data loss. Events of this type can also result in other problems, such as corruption of the operating system.

Unreliability is caused by either a low-quality, faulty or over-extended item of hardware, or problems with the operating system or a software program. Hardware is the most likely culprit, so we'll look at this first.

The PC's Power Supply

A computer has two different power supplies: the AC input from the wall socket and the DC output from the power supply unit. Both can be the source of problems that make a PC unreliable.

Even if they're OK to begin with, low-end PSUs are much more likely to develop the type of faults that affect a PC's stability.

Power Supply Unit (PSU)

These devices are prone to two types of problem and, in each case, the cause is bad design and the use of low-quality components:

in other words, they are cheap and nasty. Unfortunately, this describes the majority of PSUs supplied by PC manufacturers as part of their systems.

The first problem is that the current they supply tends to fluctuate. This means that the PC is sometimes not getting enough and at other times is getting too much. If these variations in current exceed the tolerances to which the PC's components are built, it behaves erratically.

PSUs are a part of a computer system that most people never consider; they are much more interested in the CPU speed, the video card and the amount of RAM. PC manufacturers are aware of this and use cheap PSUs to cut the cost of their systems.

The second problem is that they fail (being highly stressed components, this is inevitable), and when they do, they do it in a big way – a loud bang, accompanied by a puff of smoke.

How do you know if you have a low-quality PSU? Easy – check its specifications to see if it incorporates protection circuitry (see page 126). If it doesn't, you should replace it.

The result is a surge of current though the system that can, and does, destroy other components. Typically, these are the CPU and RAM, and sometimes the hard drive as well (where all your data is kept).

So those of you who need or want a reliable system must make sure that your current PSU is not one of these low-end affairs, and in most cases this will mean upgrading it.

There are, of course, other reasons to upgrade the PSU and these include:

- To supply the extra power requirements of new devices that the existing PSU is incapable of delivering

- To provide the power connections required by devices using new technology

Another feature offered by high-end PSUs is low-noise fans. While they are often described as being silent, in practice they aren't. They are, however, much quieter than those supplied with cheap models.

- To reduce the noise levels of the PC by taking advantage of "silent" PSUs

Whatever your reason for upgrading the PSU, considering the following factors will ensure you buy the right one.

Power Rating

The power supply unit must be capable of providing the power required by every component in the system with a bit to spare. The latter is important for two reasons:

1) The PSU (as with any device) will not last very long if it is run continuously at full load

Another specification to take note of is the PSU's efficiency rating. This is the ratio of the amount of power that goes into the PSU compared to the amount that goes out. Efficiency is expressed as a percentage and a good figure to aim at is 65%–85%.

2) Having some spare power capacity will allow you to add extra devices at a later date without also having to buy a PSU with a higher power rating

The table on the next page shows you the approximate maximum power requirements of all the components in a computer system, and will allow you to calculate the amount of power that will be required by yours.

When you've worked out how much power is required by your system, add another 50 Watts to the figure to provide some spare capacity.

Component	Power Required
Low- to mid-range video card	60 W
High-end video card	100 W
Expansion card	10 W
ATA hard drive	30 W
SATA hard drive	20 W
SCSI hard drive	40 W
Optical drive	25 W
Floppy drive	5 W
Cooling fan	2.5 W
Motherboard	35 W
256 MB RAM	15 W
High-end CPU	100 W
Low-end CPU	50 W
LED	1 W

Protection Circuitry

A good quality PSU incorporates circuits that monitor variables such as temperature and current, and if any of them exceeds designated limits, the PSU simply shuts down (rather than blowing, as cheap models do). This will, of course, also shut down the PC but no damage is done to its components. Low-end PSUs do not have this feature.

The provision of overload protection circuitry is one of the main differences between low- and high-end PSUs. Its importance cannot be overstated.

These circuits also offer some protection against fluctuations in the external AC supply, which can be another source of problems.

Cooling

Cheaper PSUs, as supplied by PC manufacturers, will have one cooling fan, which is adequate for normal operating conditions. Better-quality PSUs, however, usually have an extra fan, mounted underneath or to the side, which will kick in when the PSU is highly loaded. This provides extra cooling when it is really needed and can extend the working life of the PSU considerably.

External Power Supply

For those who are seeking system reliability, the AC supply to the PC is another factor that must be considered. External power supplies are subject to a range of faults: these include power surges, line noise and frequency variation, all of which can adversely affect the stability of a computer.

Power surges are one of the most common problems and have a similar effect on a PC as a low-quality PSU would. They also stress components and, over time, have a cumulative effect that can result in them failing well before they should.

While there is nothing that you can do about the quality of the signal, there are three levels of protection that you can employ:

1) Install a good quality PSU that has protection circuitry. This usually offers some protection against AC faults as well

2) Fit a power surge suppressor (like the one shown below). These devices "smooth out" momentary increases in the AC signal, thus ensuring the supply to the PC is at a constant level

Those of you who do mission-critical work on your PCs might consider an Uninterruptible Power Supply Unit (UPS). These units provide a battery-powered backup that takes over when the AC supply has failed. Typically, they will continue to supply power for several hours.

Courtesy of Belkin Corporation

3) Fit a Line Conditioner. These are a step up from surge suppressors and not only eliminate power surges, but eliminate electrical interference that causes line noise

For home-PC use, a top-end PSU and a power surge suppressor will ensure both a "clean" AC input to the PC, and protection against damage to other system components in the event of problems with the PSU.

Heat

Do not be tempted to remove the system case cover, or side panels, in an attempt to keep the inside cool. Cases are designed to direct cooling air to where it is needed. Removing these items will disrupt optimum air-flow and can cause pockets of warm air to build up.

Another factor that the upgrader needs to be aware of is heat, and the effect that an excess amount of it will have on the PC's components. Firstly, it stresses them beyond their design tolerances and, secondly, it makes them operate in an erratic fashion. The former causes damage and the latter causes unreliability.

Excess heat is likely to be an issue only when power-hungry devices are added to the system, the most typical example being one of the latest video cards. These devices generate serious amounts of heat and while they all come equipped with cooling systems that direct most of it out of harm's way, inevitably much of it remains in the system case. The same applies to the more recent high-end CPUs.

Cramming a lot of devices (power-hungry or not) into the case can have the same effect. For example, you may have two hard drives, a CD drive and a DVD drive, a video card, a TV tuner card, a sound card, a modem, and a SCSI or FireWire card.

In either of these situations, it may be necessary to install another cooling fan. Virtually all system cases have mounting points for these, usually located at the rear and the top.

Also available are customizable fan and air ducting systems that allow the user to direct air to precisely the place where it is needed.

In the case of a high-end video card, you may be better off fitting a PCI fan (like the one shown below). This device plugs into the PCI slot next to the video card where it is ideally situated to keep it cool.

Overheating can also be caused, or compounded, by dust blocking the out-take vents of both the PSU and the system case. A can of compressed air or a good healthy puff will clear this away. Don't forget to do the circuits boards as well; these will be covered by a layer of dust which, in case you didn't know, is an insulator.

Installing a Power Supply Unit

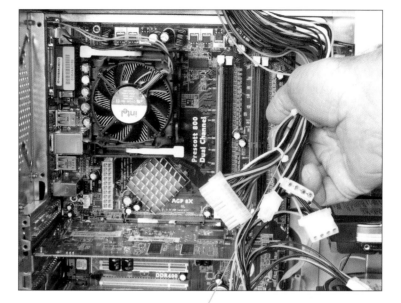

The PSU supplies four different connectors. These are:

Mainboard power

CD/hard drive power

Floppy drive power

ATX 12V

1 Disconnect the existing PSU's cables

2 Unscrew the PSU

Remember to check that the on/off switch at the rear of the new power supply unit is in the on position.

3 Remove the PSU from the case

4 Install the new PSU by reversing steps 1 to 3

Software

There are two types of software that are well known for rendering a computer system unstable and, hence, unreliable: hardware drivers and malware.

Hardware Drivers

A driver is a small program that acts as an interface between hardware and the operating system. Essentially, it's a set of instructions that tells the operating system how to control, and communicate with, the associated hardware device. In many cases, it also allows the user to make configuration changes to the device. For example, a printer driver lets you set the print quality, amongst many other things.

One of the problems with drivers is that they often contain bugs (errors), which can cause incompatibility issues with other hardware devices. This can have a knock-on effect that may result in system-wide problems, one of which is general instability.

To resolve this, hardware manufacturers periodically release updated drivers for their products in which the bugs have been fixed. So downloading and installing updated drivers for all your devices as and when they are released will minimize this cause of problems.

Malware

This term is used to describe the multitude of pesky programs that sneak themselves on to a user's PC when certain websites are visited, or are hidden in seemingly legitimate programs. These include spyware, which sends details of the user's PC back to the maker, adware, which opens advertising pop-up windows in the user's browser, and hijackers, which take over the user's browser and redirect all searches to specific sites.

Apart from being extremely irritating, these programs can have a seriously adverse effect on the performance and reliability of the PC. While it is possible to remove them (see page 184) prevention is much easier than the cure. To stop websites downloading to your PC without your knowledge, you need to install Service Pack 2 (assuming that you're running Windows XP). Also, do not install freeware and shareware programs downloaded from the Internet (see margin note).

Hardware drivers are a particularly important issue for users of Windows XP. This operating system is renowned for having compatibility problems with drivers designed for previous versions of Windows. For this reason, you should make sure that all your devices use drivers designed to work with XP.

Those of you who download free and shareware applications should be aware that in many cases the program will have an unwelcome attachment. Software, music, and movie files obtained via the file-sharing networks (Kazaa, Emule, Grokster, etc) are another source of these programs. It is essential that you scan downloads of this type with both anti-virus and malware removal programs.

Improve Your Input and Control Options

In this chapter, we look at hardware that is used either to get data into a PC, or to control it.

Controlling devices include the mouse, keyboards and game controllers. While they may seem to be straightforward with little to offer in the way of features and versatility, there are, in fact, a wide range of these devices available, many of which are designed for specific types of application, or game.

Input devices include scanners, web cameras and microphones. Everyone knows what scanners are for; what they might not know are the important specifications and features to look for.

Chapter Nine

The Mouse

Not so long ago, virtually all mice were very similar in shape and color (a bland beige), and were limited in terms of functionality. This is no longer the case; nowadays these devices are available in a range of colors and ergonomic designs that make them more interesting in a visual sense, not to mention being easier to use.

More importantly, they now use the more efficient optical technology that has replaced the old ball and wheel mechanical system. This works by using an LED (Light Emitting Diode) that bounces light off the work surface. The reflected light is processed, and if any changes are detected, the new coordinates are passed to the computer.

Unlike ball and wheel mice that need a mousemat, optical mice work on any surface that isn't highly reflective – in other words, anything except glass or similar.

LED and sensor on the underside of the mouse

The result is much smoother operation (ball and wheel mice pick up dirt that inhibits movement), and a greater degree of accuracy. Anyone still using the old-fashioned type should definitely spend the few dollars that a new optical mouse will cost.

Cordless mice can get through a lot of batteries over a period of months. For this reason, look for a model that comes with rechargeable batteries and a charging unit.

Another option is to go for a cordless mouse. These use radio frequency technology that does away with the need for a cord. Not only does this tidy up the desktop, it also allows the mouse to be used from further away. The drawback is that they are battery powered (see margin note).

Those of you who need even more accuracy have two further options. The first is the new laser mouse: these devices are a step up from standard optical mice and replace the LED with a laser beam. The MX™ 1000 from Logitech (shown below) is an example of this new breed of super-mouse.

Laser mice can be used on any type of surface; even glass doesn't faze them.

This device has some 20 times more sensitivity to surface detail (tracking power) than a standard mouse does, which makes it ideal for those who need a high level of precision. Other features include a tilting center wheel for side-to-side scrolling, cruise control for speed-scrolling up and down, and one-click zoom. All in all, a superior beast.

The second option is the trackball type of mouse. This device is basically a kind of up-ended mouse where the user positions the pointer by rotating the ball with a finger.

For applications that require a high degree of precision, laser and trackball mice are the way to go.

Apart from offering a high level of control, they are also ideal for those with hand or wrist disabilities, as they can be operated by using just a single finger.

Further advantages are that they can be used on any surface as the ball doesn't come into contact with it.

They do, however, take a bit of getting used to.

Keyboards

For general purpose use, keyboards supplied by PC manufacturers get the job done. However, they don't look anything special, their key action is not the nicest, and they have limited functionality. If you are using one of these to do serious amounts of typing, upgrading to a high-quality model is highly recommended.

One of the things you'll notice is how much more positive and responsive the action of the keys is. This is because good

For a more pleasant typing experience, go for a mechanical keyboard rather than using the cheaper membrane type.

keyboards use a mechanical key system as opposed to the membrane system used by their lesser siblings. Each key is assigned its own switch, which makes an audible click when depressed. When it is released, it springs back into place quickly.

In a membrane keyboard, all the keys sit on a sheet of plastic. This is imprinted with a metallic pattern that, when touched by a key, acts like the switch in a mechanical keyboard and sends the "key depressed" signal to the computer. This is why these keyboards have a spongy feel to them. It is also why they are much cheaper as they have many fewer parts inside them.

Also available for intensive typists is the Dvorak keyboard. These use a different key layout that is considered to be more efficient than the QWERTY layout found on standard keyboards.

Also available for serious typists are ergonomically designed keyboards. These are constructed in a way that allows users to hold their hands in a more comfortable, slightly angled, position while typing. This type of keyboard (shown below) can also help prevent, or alleviate, Carpal Tunnel Syndrome. This is an affliction that affects the wrists.

Taking this concept a bit further are split keyboards that have an adjustable hinge in the middle to vary the angle at which the keys are presented to the user's hands.

Comfort is not the only reason to upgrade a keyboard; many of these devices are tailored to meet specific user requirements. For example, those of you who frequently use Microsoft Office applications can buy models that have keys relevant to Word, PowerPoint, Excel, etc. Others have keys that control multimedia functions such as play and pause, and Internet and email functions.

Image reprinted with permission from ViewSonic Corporation

This keyboard from Viewsonic has keys for office, multimedia, Internet, and email applications

Game Controllers

PC games aficionados who need features or levels of precision not offered by the keyboard/mouse combination have four options available to them:

Gaming Keyboards

For some game genres, keyboards are the best type of controller. An example is strategy games, such as Microsoft's Age of Empires, where most of the action is controlled by the keyboard.

While standard keyboards are adequate, much better results will be had from one of the specialized gaming keyboards. These have a multitude of programmable keys that allow the user to customize the keyboard to suit specific games. Most also have an integral joystick, plus illuminated keys that allow games to be played in the dark (hardly essential, but cool nevertheless).

One of the most important features that they offer to gamers is the ability to set up macro commands that combine multiple keystrokes into one. For example, with a standard keyboard, getting a game character to jump forward and kick out simultaneously will require three keys to be pressed at the same time. A gaming keyboard will do this with one keystroke.

The Logitech® G15 Gaming Keyboard (shown right) provides a backlit, adjustable LCD that shows you crucial system information during gameplay.

Another type of gaming keyboard consists of a base unit on which can be placed customized keysets designed for use with specific games. If this interests you, visit Ideazon at www.zboard.com.

Joysticks

Joysticks are designed for use with flight simulators, although they can also be used with other genres. An important consideration with these devices is weight and build quality; joysticks are subjected to a lot of abuse and need to be up to the job physically. Another is how securely they fix to the desktop; a joystick that hops around is not going to be of much use.

More than any other type of controller, joysticks need to be securely fastened to the desktop. Consider this aspect carefully when looking at the various models.

Courtesy of Saitek

Another important feature to look for is a twist handle. This gives you rudder control in a flight game.

A good joystick will also have several programmable buttons that allow configurations to be set up for various games using the associated software.

Steering Wheels

Steering wheels are designed specifically for racing games such as Formula One and Nascar. Some even come with a pedal setup for added authenticity.

Force feedback technology creates the sense of touch and no decent controller these days would be complete without it.

One of the most important features these devices should provide is force feedback. While this is also available with other types of controller, it is particularly effective in driving games as it lets you "feel" every bump and crash.

The smoothness with which the wheel turns is something else to check – some wheels have a decidedly "clicky" feel to them.

Also, look for at least six programmable buttons, 240 degrees of wheel rotation and a secure clamping system.

GamePads

These devices are basically a cross between a wheel and a joystick as they provide features common to both but without the high level of precision. This makes them ideal for use by those who play various types of game.

Game controllers are now available in cordless versions that allows the user to sit a lot further back from the monitor. This is a particularly useful feature with gamepads, as a cord flapping about can be restrictive.

Courtesy of Saitek

Any good gamepad will provide at least eight programmable buttons, two analog joysticks (also known as thumbsticks), and a four-way D pad (used for navigation purposes). Top-end gamepads will have an eight-way D pad for more precise control.

Another consideration is the length of the cord. This should be at least six feet to give you room in which to maneuver.

Scanners

Scanners are devices that are used to import an image of a picture or document into the user's PC. The difference between low- and high-end models is the speed at which they do it, the quality of the image produced and the level of control offered.

When upgrading this device, or buying one for the first time, you need to consider the following specifications.

Scan Resolution

This is a measure of how much detail is reproduced by the scan process and is expressed in dots per inch (dpi). The higher this figure, the better the quality of the scanned image. The majority of scanners have a maximum dpi of 600 and, for most purposes, this is more than enough. Some applications require a much higher scan resolution, however, and for these, a high-end model will be needed. The following table shows what level of resolution is required by the most common applications.

Unless your images are to be printed in commercial publications, or are going to be enlarged, the highest scan resolution that you will ever need is 600 dpi.

Application	Resolution
Images for commercial printing	2400 dpi
Images to be enlarged	1200 dpi upwards
Photos for printing on inkjet printers	600 dpi
Text documents	300 dpi
Line art (drawings, diagrams, etc)	300 dpi
Images for websites	72 dpi

Interpolated resolution is basically a software enhancement of the true (hardware) resolution, and is achieved by adding extra pixels to the image. While it can improve image quality to a limited degree, it is nowhere near as good as the quoted figure may suggest. Take this with a very large pinch of salt.

When looking at a scanner's specifications, as in the example below, you may see two figures for resolution – hardware and interpolated. The hardware figure is the one you want; ignore the interpolated figure (see margin note).

Specifications

- Scanner Type — Flatbed
- Scanner Element — Charge-Coupled Device (CCD)
- Light Source — Cold Cathode Fluroescent Lamp
- Hardware Resolution — 1200 x 1200 dpi
- Interpolated Resolution — 24000 x 24000 dpi
- Color Depth — 48-bit
- Gray Scale Depth — 16-bit
- Interface Connectivity — USB 2.0
- Power Source — AC Adapter

Color Depth

This tells you how many colors the scanner can register and is measured in bits. 24 bits is the minimum required for good color reproduction. However, as virtually all scanners these days can scan at a depth of 48 bits, this isn't really an issue. It's worth checking out, though, particularly at the low end of the market.

Many scanners offer optional accessories that extend their functionality. These include slide and negative attachments, and sheet feeders.

Optical Density

Also known as Dynamic Range, this indicates how wide a range of tones the scanner can recognize, and is measured on a scale from 0.0 (perfect white) to 4.0 (perfect black).

Most flatbed scanners have an OD around 2.8-3.0 which is fine for photographs. Slides, negatives and transparencies, which have broader tonal ranges, will need a higher OD of about 3.4.

Interface

Most scanners these days use either the USB 2 or SCSI interface, both of which provide much better performance than parallel port or USB1. Note that SCSI requires a SCSI adaptor to be installed as well, so USB2 is the recommended option.

Scanners that offer one-touch buttons for common tasks can save you a lot of time.

Scanning Area

Most flatbed scanners are large enough to scan at letter size. Larger documents will require a scanner with a correspondingly bigger scanning area (and price).

Web Cameras

Traditionally, the only practical uses for these devices have been video links for conferencing purposes, and recording video "greeting cards" to send to friends and family.

Web cameras are well known for the poor quality video they produce. If you need a clearer image, you may need to buy an Internet camera, as shown below.

However, thanks to the current ease and affordability of setting up a home wireless network (see page 160), there is now another way to employ them.

In conjunction with a wireless network and a basic software program, a handful of these devices can be used to create a flexible and low-cost home surveillance system. This can be used for a multitude of purposes, such as detecting intruders and keeping an eye on the baby. It can also be easily extended or relocated; for example, moving a camera outdoors to make sure the guys relaying the drive are doing the job properly.

Microphones

Many Internet telephony companies are now offering low-cost, or even free, Internet calls for people using their software. An example is Skype at www.skype.com.

Microphones are used as a means of getting the spoken word into a PC. Typical uses are dubbing home movies and voice recognition. They can also be used in conjunction with a PC for voice links over the Internet.

The latter (known as Internet Telephony) has been around for a while now, but technical issues that have resulted in poor quality connections and unreliability have prevented it from taking off. However, while still far from perfect, the technology behind it has now improved to the extent that it is now a serious option, particularly for overseas calls.

For general use, a high-quality microphone is not necessary. However, you should get a directional model as opposed to omnidirectional, particularly if you are going to use it for voice recognition. The latter kind picks up background sounds while the directional type doesn't.

Internet telephony is now being seen as the next major communications revolution and all that's required is a PC, a microphone of reasonable quality, and a software program.

Data Output Options

The two devices used to present a computer's data are the monitor and the printer. Monitors are available using either CRT or the increasingly popular LCD technology. While the latter offer some quite compelling reasons to buy them, they do have limitations that the upgrader should be aware of. In some respects, CRT monitors are a better option.

Printers suitable for PCs also come in two types – inkjet and laser. Plus, there are photo printers, which are basically an enhanced version of the inkjet. The pros and cons of all three, and the applications they are suitable for, are discussed in this chapter.

Covers

Chapter Ten

Monitors – CRT versus LCD

There are two types of CRT monitor – Shadow Mask and Aperture Grille. Of the two, the Aperture Grille type is the best.

These devices use one of two technologies – Cathode Ray Tube (CRT) and Liquid Crystal Display (LCD). Each has its own inherent strengths and weaknesses, which make it suitable for some applications and less so for others. Choosing between the two is the first decision the upgrader has to make, and to ensure the correct decision is made, the following factors must be considered.

Courtesy of Samsung

Supported Resolutions

A monitor's resolution is the number of pixels that comprise the image, and it is expressed in terms of width x height. Commonly used resolutions are 1024 x 768, 1280 x 1024 and 1600 x 1200.

Due to the way manufacturers measure screen size, LCD monitors have a larger viewing area than equivalent CRTs. For example, a 17-inch LCD has a screen size of 17 inches, while a 17-inch CRT has a screen size of 16 inches, or even less.

CRT monitors are able to support all of these, plus others, at a high level of image quality. An LCD, however, can support only one resolution at high quality. This is known as its native resolution. While it can support others, they are achieved by using interpolation techniques that result in a much lower quality display.

What this all boils down to is that if you run applications that require different resolutions, a CRT has to be the choice. For example, gamers find that certain games play better at one resolution than they do at others and vice versa. However, if the native resolution provided by a specific LCD is acceptable for all your applications, this won't be an issue and your choice will be determined by other factors.

An LCD monitor will be suitable only if its native resolution is adequate for all your applications.

Response Time

This is a measure of how long it takes a monitor to respond to changes in the display. This is a very important factor when playing movies or games because a slow response time can cause a ghosting effect, which can spoil the display. With CRTs, this isn't an issue as their response time is almost instantaneous. LCDs, however, react much more slowly.

The bottom line here is that if you want to watch video on an LCD, its response time must be 16 ms or lower. Many LCDs currently on the market have a response time well above this figure, so this is something that you must check out in the specifications.

For smooth, fluid playback of video, an LCD monitor must have a response time of 16 ms or less.

Courtesy of Samsung

Image Quality
This is defined as clarity and color reproduction. Here, honours are about even. LCDs produce an image of startling clarity and crispness that CRTs cannot match (although many people prefer the softer look of a CRT display).

In terms of color reproduction, CRTs can display a wider range of colors than LCDs. This makes them more suitable for those who work with graphics, or indeed, any application in which accurate color reproduction is important.

Ergonomics

LCDs are much easier on the eye. Users who spend long periods at the PC will benefit from this.

The image on a CRT has to be "refreshed" by continuously redrawing it by means of an electron beam that sweeps from the top to the bottom of the screen. This can produce a faintly perceptible flickering that causes eye fatigue and headaches if the user is over-exposed to it.

LCDs do not suffer from this problem as they use a flat matrix display where every pixel is always active. Furthermore, LCDs have a more uniform screen brightness that results in considerably less glare compared to CRTs.

Viewing Angle
CRTs can be viewed from any angle and, while the sharper the angle the less you can see, the image itself doesn't deteriorate.

Good quality LCDs have a viewing angle of 160 to 170 degrees. Low-end models have viewing angles as low as 60 degrees.

This is not the case with LCDs. With these, there is a noticeable loss of image quality when the monitor is viewed from an angle. It is not a major issue but it is, nevertheless, there.

Physical Dimensions

One of the biggest advantages of LCDs is their depth – typically two to three inches – as opposed to some 17 inches for a 17-inch CRT. This allows them to be pushed much further back, thus creating more usable desk space. It also makes them much lighter, and thus easier to transport.

Power Requirements

LCD monitors are much more efficient in terms of energy consumption. The power required for these devices is about a third of that for CRTs. A welcome side-effect of this is that they produce less heat.

Radiation

CRT monitors do emit a certain amount of low-frequency radiation. Some people think this can be harmful; others don't. If you use an LCD monitor, the issue becomes irrelevant as these devices emit virtually no radiation.

Dead Pixels

With some LCDs it is possible to pivot the display from landscape to portrait. This is an option that can be useful in some types of application, e.g. graphics and CAD.

Other LCDs can be detached from the stand and fixed to a wall. While we can't think of an obvious use for this feature, someone, somewhere, no doubt will find one.

Pixels are tiny elements that, together, form the display of a monitor. With LCDs, if a pixel is damaged and thus doesn't work, it stands out from the ones that surround it as a dot of a different color. This was a considerable problem with early LCDs and buyers were expected to accept a number of dead pixels.

These days, this is less of an issue as LCD technology has improved. However, it is still common to get an LCD with one or two dead pixels and so it is worth finding out what a manufacturer's policy is regarding this before parting with the cash. Many will replace the monitor but some won't.

Cost

While LCDs have come down in price dramatically in recent years, they are still slightly more expensive than a CRT offering a similar level of performance and features.

Important Monitor Specifications

To ensure that your monitor is capable of doing what you require of it, the following specifications are the ones to take note of.

LCD Monitors

Resolution. The first thing to look at is the monitor's native, or fixed, resolution; this must be suitable for your applications. Note that this will also determine the size of the monitor. 15-inch monitors have a native resolution of 1024 x 768, 17- and 19-inch monitors 1280 x 1024, 20- and 21-inch monitors 1600 x 1200, and 23-inch monitors 1920 x 1200. So, for example, if you need, or are comfortable, with a resolution of 1280 x 1024, your choice will be restricted to 17- and 19-inch models.

Response Rate. If you intend to play games or watch movies, the monitor must have a response rate no higher than 16 ms. Otherwise, the quality of the display will be compromised in the form of a ghosting or streaking effect.

Contrast Ratio. This is the measurement of the difference in light intensity between the brightest (white) and darkest (black) tones, and provides a good indicator of an LCD's image quality. If it is too low, the image will look faded and washed out, whereas a high contrast ratio will result in an image that is vibrant and colorful. The lowest figure you should accept is 350:1. High-quality LCDs will have a ratio nearer to 600:1.

CRT Monitors

Dot Pitch. This is a measure of the distance between individual pixels and is the best indicator of a CRT's image quality. The lower the figure, the greater the sharpness and color clarity of the displayed image. High quality models will have a dot pitch around 0.21 mm, while low-end models will be around 0.28 mm. 0.26 mm provides a reasonable picture; monitors with a higher dot pitch should be avoided.

Resolution. This is a less important specification than it is with LCDs, as CRTs can handle many different resolutions. However, if you need high resolutions (1600 x 1200 and above), you will require a large monitor (a minimum of 19 inches, preferably bigger). Otherwise, you will need a magnifying glass to read the display as it will be so small.

When buying an LCD monitor, make sure it has a DVI input (see page 110). This will allow it to accept a digital signal from your video card, which will improve the quality of the display.

A CRT monitor's dot pitch rating is the most important specification regarding its visual quality. Note that this is not an important specification with LCDs.

Installing a Monitor

CRT Monitors

These use the blue VGA connection and connect either to the video card or to the motherboard's integrated video system.

If your PC has both a video card and integrated video, make sure that you connect the monitor to the right one. This is a very common mistake and is easily done.

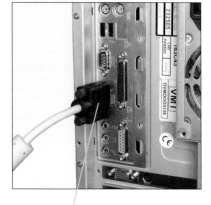

Video card connection

Integrated video connection

LCD Monitors

These can use both VGA and DVI connections. If your system has a DVI-equipped video card, this is the one to use. Otherwise, use the VGA connection as shown above.

If your LCD monitor has both VGA and DVI inputs, you can use it with two separate PCs. Connect one PC via the VGA input and the other via the DVI input. The monitor will have a control that lets you switch between the two.

DVI output from the video card

Printers

To meet their printing requirements, upgraders have a choice of four types of device. These are:

- Inkjet printers
- Laser printers
- Photo printers
- Multi-function devices (MFDs)

Inkjet Printers

Cheap and readily available, these devices are the ideal solution for all-round, or occasional, printing requirements. Print quality, while not the best, is perfectly adequate for most purposes.

Manufacturers rate the print speed of their printers in pages per minute (PPM). However, these are taken under optimal printing conditions and do not reflect their real-world performance. Take these with a pinch of salt – the real print speed will be considerably less.

They do, however, have some limitations that make them unsuitable for high-quality or large-scale printing.

If you do serious amounts of printing, an inkjet will be a slow and expensive way of doing it.

- Inkjets are not the quickest printers; in fact many of them are painfully slow at anything other than draft quality. For the odd letter now and then they are fine, but for more serious printing, the slow print speed can be very restrictive.

- Inkjets may be available at low prices but this definitely does not apply to the consumables (ink cartridges, paper, etc). These are highly priced and this is where the manufacturers make their money.

● Inkjets can be messy devices because they work by literally firing the ink at the paper. It is quite common with these devices for ink to contaminate the platen and rollers, which then transfer it to the paper in the form of unwanted smudges and streaks.

Should you decide to buy one of these printers, consider the following:

Print Resolution. This is expressed in dots per inch (dpi). Letter quality will require a resolution of 600 dpi, while photographs need one of 1200 dpi. Most current inkjets are capable of the latter but it will be worth checking if you do intend to print photos.

Print Speed. This is rated in pages per minute (PPM) and, as we mentioned on the previous page, it does not give an accurate indication. However, it can be useful as a rough guide when comparing different models.

Paper Handling. Mainstream inkjets will print letter size or lower. If you need to print larger documents, you will need to buy a business class inkjet, which will be considerably more expensive. Another thing to look at if you envisage having long print jobs, is the capacity of the paper input tray. Low-end inkjets will hold no more than 50 sheets or so; high-end models will hold about 150.

Photo Printers

With the increasing use of PCs for storing and editing images, photo printers are now extremely popular. These also use inkjet

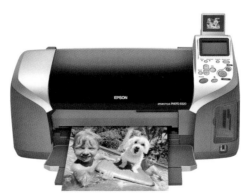

technology but take it to a different level in terms of print quality. One of the ways they achieve this is by using a wider range of colored inks than standard inkjets do. As a result, print quality approaches that of professional print labs.

Not all printers with the word "photo" in their name are actually photo printers. Some are merely a general-purpose printer with a few photo printer features, such as direct printing from memory cards or the ability to make borderless prints. Study the specs carefully to weed out the jokers.

Photo printers are also much quicker than standard inkjets, which can take an eternity to print a high-quality photo. Another feature they offer is the ability to read directly from flash memory cards, such as those used by digital cameras. This means that the PC is bypassed completely. Many also offer an LCD to view your photos, not to mention editing facilities such as cropping, rotation, and brightness and contrast adjustment.

Things to look out for when buying a photo printer include:

Ink Cartridges. Photo printers use between four and six different inks and, generally, the ones that use six will produce higher quality prints than those that use fewer.

You should also be aware that some use a single cartridge that contains all the inks, so if one color runs out, the cartridge has to be replaced even though the other colors haven't. Therefore, running costs can be cut substantially by choosing a model in which each color is held in a separate cartridge.

PictBridge is a standardized technology that lets you transfer images from the memory card in a digital camera directly to a printer. Print size, layout, date, and other settings can be set within the camera. However, both the printer and the camera must support PictBridge.

Memory Card Reader. If you want to take advantage of the direct printing facility offered by these printers, make sure it can read the type of memory card that you use. In particular, look for PictBridge support (see margin note).

Print Size. Most photo printers have a maximum print size of 4 x 6 inches, which is fine for snapshots. If you want larger sizes, say to frame and hang on the wall, you will need to buy a more expensive model.

Laser Printers

Lasers use a completely different technology, which produces better print quality and higher speed than inkjets. They also offer much more in the way of features, such as duplexing (the ability to print on both sides of the page) and high-capacity paper input trays. Furthermore, they have much lower running costs.

Traditionally, these devices have been superb at printing text but not so good at color images, as print resolutions were often limited to 600 dpi (which is fine for text). However, with more and more users demanding photo quality from their laser printers, the manufacturers are now providing models that print at 1200 dpi.

One useful advantage provided by color lasers over inkjets is the ability to print high-quality photos on plain paper – expensive glossy paper is not necessary.

While these do produce good-quality color prints, it must be said that low-end color lasers still cannot match an inkjet photo printer. Models that can will cost more than $1000 US.

Courtesy of Samsung

The price of laser printers has dropped considerably over the last couple of years and it is now possible to buy a black and white model for around $200 US, which is less than a high-end inkjet will cost. However, prospective buyers should be aware that if they buy one of these low-cost models, they will be buying at the bottom of the laser market and the performance offered may be no better than that of a good quality inkjet. Probably the only benefit will be lower running costs.

Keep your eyes peeled for laser printers that claim an "effective" resolution of 1200 dpi. This means a real resolution of 600 dpi that has been bumped up by means of software enhancement. This is a way (much favored by manufacturers of printers and scanners), to make products appear better than they actually are.

When buying a laser printer, consider the following:

Print Resolution. For text, a dpi of 600 is fine. However, if you intend to print color photos, a dpi of 1200 is recommended. Note that low-end color lasers offer a dpi of only 600.

Consumables. While these are much cheaper than inkjet consumables, you can make further savings by buying a model that has the toner (laser equivalent to inkjet ink) in a separate cartridge. Some lasers have the toner and the drum (which needs to be replaced much less frequently) combined in a single cartridge. As the toner runs out long before it is necessary to replace the drum, being able to replace each individually is more cost-effective.

Memory. Lasers come equipped with their own memory. However, low-end models aren't equipped with much, often only enough for small-scale print jobs and low-resolution photo printing. Make sure that the model you buy allows you to install extra memory (not all do), should it be necessary.

Multi-Function Devices (MFDs)

These devices consist of a printer and a scanner, which also combine to act as a copier, and sometimes a fax machine, all incorporated within the same housing.

A potential problem with multi-function devices is that, if they go wrong, the user may lose all the functions that they provide.

The advantages offered are convenience (one connection to the PC, one wall socket required), less desktop space than would be required by stand-alone devices, and a cost saving compared to buying the devices separately.

Along with the lower price, however, you will usually also get lower quality, unless you opt for a high-end model, in which case you will lose the cost saving. The advice then is to steer clear of MFDs unless: a) space is at a premium, and b) you can afford a high-end model that will meet your requirements. To this end, you should study the specifications for each incorporated device as you would with stand-alone devices.

The bottom line, then, is:

- For high-quality glossy photographs, an inkjet photo printer will be the best choice, unless you are prepared to shell out $1000-plus for a mid-range color laser. If high-quality text printing is also a requirement, it might be necessary to buy a high-end standard inkjet, or low-end laser printer, as well

- For large-scale text-based print jobs, a black and white laser is the recommended option. Even a low-end model will be better than most inkjets, with the added advantage of much lower running costs

- For the busy home office where print jobs are frequent, and you use both text and color, a low-end color laser will be a real boon. Not only will printing be quicker and cheaper; more options will be available, such as being able to print on both sides of a page. In short, productivity will be much increased

- If space and/or cost is an issue, and high quality isn't, go for a multi-function device

Installing a Printer

Printers are very simple devices to install.

Parallel Port Printers

The first step is to switch the PC off – parallel port devices cannot be installed while the PC is running.

When installing a parallel port printer, the PC must be switched off. This is not the case with USB models, as USB devices are "hot swappable".

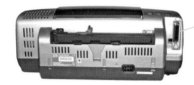

Locate the printer's parallel port socket

Note that with some parallel port printers, the driver must be installed before the device is connected to the PC – read the instructions.

1   Connect one end of the interface cable to the printer

2   Connect the other end to the PC's parallel port

USB Printers

These devices can be installed while the PC is on.

As soon as you have connected your USB printer, Windows will see it, ask for the installation disk, and install the driver automatically.

With parallel port printers, versions of Windows prior to XP will not do this – you have to tell Windows that you have just added a printer by installing the driver manually.

1   Simply connect the USB cable to a USB port on the PC

Better Network Connections

As anyone who's upgraded an Internet connection from dial-up to broadband will tell you, the difference it makes to your use of the Internet is dramatic. We see why this is so, and also what types of broadband are available.

Even if you elect to stay with the dial-up method of connection, there are gains to be had by upgrading to the latest type of dial-up modem.

Home networking is an option available to all but used by few. We take a look at the benefits it offers, types of network and how to build them.

Covers

Chapter Eleven

Dial-Up Connections

Those of you using dial-up modems for your Internet connection have two ways of improving your connection speed. The first is by upgrading to broadband, which we'll look at on page 156.

we'll look at on page 156.

All dial-up modems are built to a specific standard. These are prefaced by the letter V, and range from V.13, the earliest standard, to the current one, V.92.

The second is to upgrade your existing dial-up modem. Whether this is worth doing or not depends on the age of your PC. If it is three years or more old, you will definitely gain by doing so. If it is less than three years old, you may already have the latest type.

In the former case, your modem will probably be a V.90 model (see top margin note), which means that it is capable of operating at 56 Kb/s. This is currently the maximum speed for modems, so an upgrade will not increase your connection speed. However, it will allow you to take advantage of the benefits offered by the latest modem standard, V.92 (see bottom margin note). If you have a really old PC, the modem could well be a V.34 model, which will have a speed of 33.6 Kb/s. In this case, an upgrade will improve your connection speed as well.

PCs less than three years old should already have V.92 modems (this standard was introduced in 2003). However, it is worth checking that yours actually does.

The V.92 standard does not offer any speed increases over V.90. However, it does offer the following improvements:

• Quick Connect – this halves the time needed to establish a connection

• Modem-on-hold – this allows the user to make outgoing, and take incoming, telephone calls without breaking the Internet connection

• Upload Speed – this is increased from 33 Kb/s to 44 Kb/s

The issue of connection speed apart, there are other reasons to upgrade. One is to use your PC as a fax machine, which will require a fax enabled modem (most modems supplied by PC manufacturers aren't). Another is to set up a telephone answering machine on the PC; this will require a voice modem.

Upgrading a PCI card modem to an external modem will release the PCI socket for another device. A further advantage is that external modems have a number of LEDs, which can be useful when troubleshooting connection problems.

Installing a Dial-Up Modem

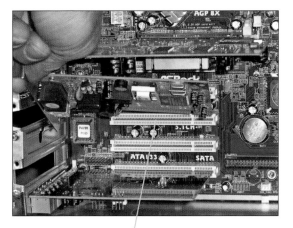

Slide the modem into a PCI slot

Press it home

To complete the installation, install the modem's driver when back in Windows.

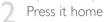

3 Connect one end of the cable to the modem's output socket and

4 Connect the other end to the telephone jack

Broadband Connections

The advantages offered by broadband provide the most compelling reason to throw away the dial-up modem. Here are just some:

If you have a need for speed, broadband is the way to go.

Accessibility. With an always-on connection, the Internet becomes literally an extension of the PC. Any site can be accessed with just a couple of mouse clicks.

Reliability. Broadband offers a far more reliable connection than dial-up modems do.

Speed. Downloads with broadband take a fraction of the time needed by dial-up connections. General web navigation is also far quicker.

Telephone. You will be able to make and take telephone calls without having to log off.

Having made the decision to do it, the first step is to sign up to one of the packages offered by your ISP. Next, you need to acquire a broadband modem. Here, you have two options: a) buy the modem yourself, or b) rent the modem from the ISP. The third step will be the ISP sending a technician round to hook you up to the network. If you are renting the modem, the technician will install it for you during the same visit. Otherwise, you'll have to install it yourself.

If you are fortunate enough to have a choice, cable broadband is the recommended option. It's quick, reliable, and easy to set up.

You also need to consider the various types of broadband as they all have their pros and cons. The most common is ADSL, as this uses the telephone network. As long as your local exchange is suitably equipped, this will be available. The same applies to ISDN; however, this offers much slower speeds.

The best option, if it's available, is cable. This utilizes CATV cable networks and offers speeds of up to 3 Mb/s. It is also the most reliable as most cables are undergound where they are not subject to storm and other types of damage. The next best option is ADSL, which offers speeds similar to cable but is not as reliable. ISDN is the least attractive option as speeds are limited to a maximum of 128 Kb/s.

The only real disadvantage of broadband is that it is a little more expensive than dial-up.

Installing a Broadband Modem

The first step is to extend the signal input from the point where it enters the house to the place where the modem is located. For this

you will need a suitable length of coaxial cable and the appropriate connectors. If you are tapping into your TV's cable input, you will also need a signal splitter, as shown left. Connect the signal cable to the splitter's input, the TV to one output and the modem's cable to the other. Then run the latter to the modem.

If you are using an Ethernet modem, you will also need an Ethernet adaper in the PC. There may be one built in to the motherboard, in which case you will have to install the Ethernet driver from the motherboard's installation disk. Otherwise, you will need to buy and install a separate adapter.

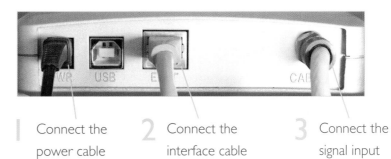

1 Connect the power cable

2 Connect the interface cable

3 Connect the signal input

When running your new modem for the first time, remember that it may need several minutes to synchronize itself with the network. During this period, you will be unable to access the Internet.

4 Connect the modem (a USB modem in this example) to the PC. An Ethernet modem will connect to an Ethernet adaptor PCI card

5 Switch the PC on and, when Windows has restarted, run the installation disk. In the case of a USB modem, the USB driver required by the modem will be installed automatically. The software will then establish and configure your broadband connection

Home Networking

A network consists of a number of computers that are inter-connected by either a cable (when it's known as a wired network) or a radio link (when it's known as a wireless network). Any type, or combination, of computers can be used in this way. It is also possible to add devices such as printers to extend the versatility of the network.

A wireless network adaptor. Courtesy of D-Link, Inc

The users of networked PCs have direct access to all the other PCs on the network, thus allowing the contents and resources of each PC to be shared. So if user A needs a file that is on user B's PC, it can be simply copied across. This is extremely convenient. If only one of the PCs has a printer connected to it, all the other PC users can use this printer; this is very cost-effective.

In a home environment, a network brings many advantages. One is the facility to share a single Internet connection between a number of PCs located in different rooms. A good example of this in use is the kids using the Internet to do their homework. Son and daughter can each engage in this activity without having to wait for the other to finish. At the same time, Dad can be checking his emails or catching up on the baseball results. The inevitable conflicts that would otherwise arise from having to share the connection are eliminated.

If the network is wireless, it is much more flexible. For example, if it's a nice day you can take your laptop out into the garden and work from there. PCs can be moved to different locations without having to re-route cabling. Wireless hotspots (see margin note) enable the user to access the network from literally anywhere in the world.

The advantages and uses provided by a home network are clear. What will be less clear to most people is how to set one up. To find out how it's done, read on.

Building a Home Network

Wired Networks

The traditional method is by using specialized network cable that connects to a network adapter in each of the networked PCs. With large networks, such as are found in corporate environments, this is no easy task as it requires a thorough knowledge of network topology (types of configuration and associated pros and cons), and devices such as routers and access points.

Network cable is approximately a quarter of an inch in diameter, so don't think that you will be able to get away with running it under the carpets.

In a home environment, though, it is a relatively straightforward task as each PC is simply linked to the next one. The main problem involves the routing of the cable. If you are handy with an electric drill, and are comfortable with the prospect of pulling up floorboards and recessing the cable into the walls, go ahead. No matter how handy you are, though, a certain amount of redecorating will be necessary.

The advantages of this type of network are speed and reliability. Network cable offers the fastest possible data transfer speeds, and once in place, the system will be extremely reliable as the cable is durable, and also shielded against electrical interference. The only thing that's likely to go wrong is a dodgy connection to one of the PCs, which is easily and quickly remedied.

Power Cable Networks

A much easier, and less messy, system, known as HomePlug, uses the house's power cables. This is available in kits consisting of two or more HomePlug adapters, an installation CD and all the

HomePlug networks generally run at approximately 14 Mb/s. Compare this with 100 Mb/s for cable networks and 54 Mb/s for wireless networks. If all you want is to share an Internet connection, and simple file sharing, they are adequate. However, they do not provide enough bandwidth for sharing audio and video files.

Having said that, Devolo (www.devolo.com) offer a high speed Homeplug kit that can run as fast as 85 Mb/s.

necessary connection cables. All you have to do is plug each adapter into the nearest wall socket, connect them to network adapters in the PCs and run the installation CD. As most rooms have at least one wall socket, there should be no need to install any wiring at all, apart from maybe an extension cable from the socket to the PC.

Telephone Wire Networks

A system very similar to Homeplug, called HomePNA, makes use of the telephone wiring in the house. Again, this is supplied in kits comprising a number of adapters, connection cables and software.

HomePNA networks are the slowest of all the various types, at 10 Mb/s. Accordingly, they are only suitable for very basic networks.

The ease of setting it up depends on whether you have telephone jacks near enough to the PCs to be networked. If you don't, though, they are simple enough to install with the aid of extension kits. Plus, the cables can be run under carpets.

Wireless Networks

Also known as Wi-Fi, this is the easiest way to set up a home network, assuming that you are running Windows XP. A wireless network can be set up with other operating systems but it is a more difficult and protracted procedure. The network wizard provided by XP does the job with a few clicks of the mouse.

All that's required in the way of hardware is a wireless network adapter for each PC to be networked. This can be either an internal PCI card or an external USB device.

An issue that ought to be considered with regard to wireless networks is that of security. Anyone with suitable radio equipment can easily hack into an unprotected wireless network. While it's unlikely to happen in a home environment, if you do have sensitive data (work documents, for example) on your PC, you should add a layer of protection.

The best method of doing this is to add a hardware firewall to the network, which will block access to it. Another method is data encryption, which can be set up with Windows XP.

Apart from the ease of setting them up, the great advantages of wireless networks are their flexibility, and the range of uses to which they can be put. With regard to the latter, there are now any number of wireless devices on the market, such as LCD TVs, music systems, and cameras.

By incorporating them into a wireless network, these devices can simply be picked up and moved to wherever they are needed.

Repairing Your PC

There are a million and one things that can go wrong with a computer and we simply haven't the space to describe them all here. So in the main, the faults highlighted in this chapter are restricted to the ones most likely to be experienced as a result of a component upgrade.

As XP is currently the most popular operating system, the screenshots and troubleshooting procedures (where applicable) are taken from this version of Windows.

Covers

Initial Steps

In practice, it is virtually impossible to repair a hardware device, particularly circuit boards, such as motherboards and video cards. To do so would require specialized electronic equipment, e.g. an oscilloscope, plus the knowledge of how to use it.

Faults with hardware devices are actually very rare. In most cases, the problem will be caused by a software issue, such as a corrupted or incorrect driver.

Because of this, computer hardware is normally repaired by the simple expedient of replacement with a working model. This is what repair technicians do and it is dead easy – the difficult part is pin-pointing the faulty component.

One reason for this is the fact that many PC faults can have several causes and this makes it difficult to know where to start. A very useful pointer here is that the majority of faults are actually induced by the user, often as a result of doing something incorrectly, or doing something that shouldn't have been done at all.

So the first thing to do is cast your mind back to what you were doing on the PC prior to the fault materializing. Very often this will provide you with a starting point. The following activities are the cause of most problems.

Installing and Uninstalling Software
Software installation can introduce bugs, and incompatibility issues with other software, particularly the operating system. Uninstalling software can also uninstall files needed by other programs.

When troubleshooting a PC, it is essential to have a planned line of attack. Going at it like a bull in a china store will almost always make matters worse.

Using the Internet and Email
The Internet can introduce malware, and email can introduce viruses.

Installing Hardware
Hardware drivers are renowned for causing configuration problems with other hardware devices. If the hardware is an internal device, it can also be the cause of heat issues. Dislodging the connections of other components during the installation is another potential cause of problems.

Changing BIOS and System Settings
This can cause a whole range of faults.

Incorrect Shutting Down of the PC
This can corrupt the PC's file system, and Windows startup files.

Troubleshooting Tools

Before you do any upgrading, you should familiarize yourself with the diagnostic and repair tools provided by Windows in case of subsequent problems.

System Restore

Versions of Windows from Me onwards provide a utility called System Restore. This utility takes "snapshots" (called restore points) of the entire system whenever major changes are made to it, such as a program being installed or uninstalled. These snapshots are saved and can be used to restore the system to the state it was in when the snapshot was taken.

This is an extremely useful way of repairing a fault without having to go to the bother of locating it, and will resolve many software issues. Obviously, it cannot repair a faulty hardware device and if you are certain that hardware is the problem, there is no point in running it. Otherwise, System Restore should be your first move.

System Restore should be used whenever you suspect the fault is software related. Hardware faults, unfortunately, are not so easily resolved.

1 Go to Start, All Programs, Accessories, System Tools, System Restore

2 At the first screen, click "Restore my computer to an earlier time"

One caveat with System Restore that you should be aware of is that any programs installed since the restore point was taken will be uninstalled by the restoration procedure. This applies to hardware as well, i.e. the drivers will be uninstalled. Your data, however, will be kept.

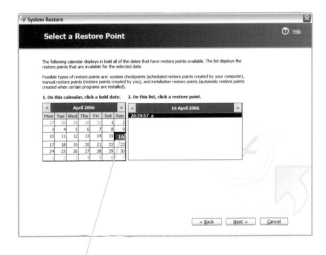

3 Select an appropriate restore point and click Next. Windows will restore the system and then reboot to complete the procedure

Device Manager

Technically, this is not a troubleshooting tool. However, it does indicate when a hardware device has a problem, and so can be very useful. Access the utility as follows:

If you suspect a hardware fault, the Device Manager is the first place to go. Very often the problem will be a corrupted driver and Device Manager will tell you if this is the case. You will also be able to reinstall the driver from here.

1 Go to Start, Control Panel, System. Click the Hardware tab and then click Device Manager

2 Here you see a list of every hardware device installed on the PC

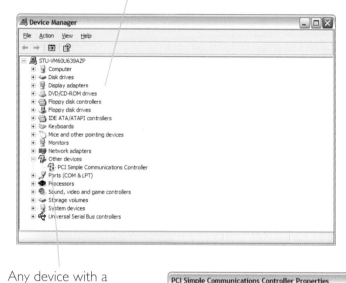

Any device that has a problem is marked with a warning symbol in Device Manager.

3 Any device with a problem will have a warning symbol next to it

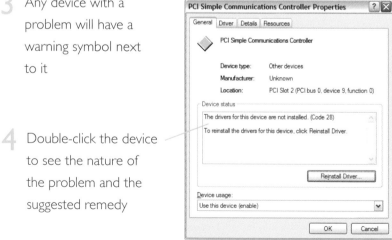

4 Double-click the device to see the nature of the problem and the suggested remedy

Safe Mode

Safe Mode is used to troubleshoot problems that prevent Windows from starting. It works by bypassing the normal Windows configuration, and instead loading a "stripped-down" version with a set of basic drivers. This eliminates many potential problems and will usually get Windows running. You are then able to access Windows troubleshooting tools, which will enable you to locate the source of the problem. Access Safe Mode as follows:

If you are unable to get Windows started, reboot the PC into Safe Mode; this should get it going. However, be aware that when in Safe Mode, Windows will run much more slowly than usual and many of its functions will be disabled. Its troubleshooting tools, such as System Restore and Device Manager, will be accessible, though.

1 Boot the PC and immediately start tapping the F8 key. After a few moments, the Windows Advanced Options Menu will open

```
Windows Advanced Options Menu
Please select An Option

Safe Mode
Safe Mode With Networking
Safe Mode With Command Prompt

Enable Boot Logging
Enable VGA Mode
Last Known Good Configuration (Yout Most Recent Settings That Worked)
Directory Services Restore Mode (Windows Domain Controllers Only)

Start Windows Normally
Reboot
Return To OS Choices Menu

Use the up and down arrow keys to move the highlight to your choice
```

Chkdsk should also be run after an incorrect shutdown has occurred. This is the most common cause of file system errors.

2 Using the arrow keys, scroll to Safe Mode and press Enter. Unless there is a serious problem with Windows itself, it will now start

Chkdsk

Chkdsk is a utility that checks the hard drive for physical errors, such as bad sectors and, more importantly, errors in the PC's file system. It will also repair any problems that it finds. Good indicators of a corrupted file system are general system instability, file copy errors and loss of data. Whenever you experience any of these problems, you should run Chkdsk.

Users of Windows 95, 98 and Me do not have Chkdsk. These systems provide a tool known as Scandisk, which does the same thing. Access it by going to Start, Programs, Accessories, System Tools.

To do it, open My Computer and right-click the C: drive. Select Properties and then click the Tools tab. Under Error checking, click Check Now and then in the new window check "Automatically fix file system errors". Then click Start.

Make a Windows XP Boot Disk

Your Windows XP boot disk will enable you to resolve the following problems:

- *A damaged boot sector*
- *A damaged master boot record (MBR)*
- *Missing or corrupt Ntldr or Ntdetect.com files*
- *A corrupt Ntbootdd.sys driver*

A PC refusing to start is one of the most soul-destroying things that can happen to a user, and most people have no idea of what to do about it. Nine times out of ten, the cause is a corrupted startup file and while there is a way of resolving this within Windows, it is far from easy. A much simpler way is to use a boot disk that you have made earlier containing copies of critical startup files. To use it, all you have to do is place it in the floppy drive and reboot the PC. Windows will then use the good file on the disk to get itself going. To make a boot disk:

1   Place a blank formatted floppy disk in the floppy drive and then go to My Computer. Click the hard drive, and on the toolbar click Tools, Folder Options. Then click the View tab

2   Scroll down and check "Show hidden files and folders." A bit further down, uncheck "Hide protected operating system files (recommended)". Click OK. Some grayed-out files will now be visible in the drive window; these are protected system files

Should you ever have occasion to use your boot disk, don't forget to replace the startup files on the hard drive with copies from the boot disk. Otherwise, you'll have the same problem every time you boot the PC.

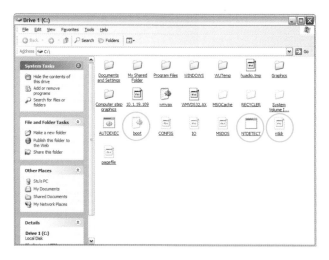

3   Select the boot, NTDETECT and ntldr files. Then right-click, click Send To, and select 3½ Floppy (A:). When the files have been transferred, your boot disk is complete. Label it and put it somewhere safe

The Power Supply

As we have mentioned previously, power supply units are one of the hardware devices most likely to cause trouble. Usually, they leave the user in no doubt – there's a loud bang accompanied by a wisp of smoke, which is pretty conclusive. However, nothing in life is certain, so if your PC appears to be dead, you have to check the power supply first, bang or no bang.

PSU faults are not always apparent. As we explained on pages 124–125, these devices can be the cause of fluctuating current to the PC. If you are experiencing an abnormal number of system crashes or lock-ups, the PSU is one of the first things to check.

Before you do, establish that the PC really is dead. There are three things to check:

1) The LEDs at the front of the case are all off

2) The keyboard LEDs are off

3) The power supply unit and CPU fans are not running

If none of the above are working then the PC is not receiving any power. Troubleshoot by checking the following:

- Confirm that there is power at the wall socket by plugging an appliance such as a hairdryer into it. If the appliance works, the socket is OK

- Bypass any device that is connected between the wall socket and the PSU, such as a surge suppressor or cable extension

- Check the PC's power cable by replacing it with one known to be good (you may have a household appliance that uses the same type)

Don't overlook the on/off switch on the PSU. What's out of sight is often out of mind. Many users are not even aware that it exists.

- Check that the on/off switch at the rear of the PSU hasn't been switched to the off position inadvertently. This is not unlikely if small children have been in the vicinity recently

If the computer is still not powering up after you have carried out these checks, the power supply unit has failed and will have to be replaced.

System Hardware

By system hardware, we mean hardware devices without which the PC will not start. These are:

- The motherboard
- Memory
- The video system

As far as the upgrader is concerned, problems with any of these devices will probably be restricted to connection issues. The beep codes will tell you which device has a problem; just check the relevant connections.

If any of these is faulty, bootup will stop at the first boot screen. Depending on which one is at fault, and the type of fault, you may see text on the screen or you may see nothing at all. However, you will *hear* something and this is your clue as to what's going on.

The sound you hear will be a series of beeps, which are known as beep codes because they have a meaning. Each code is different and indicates a fault (usually non-specific) with one of the devices. Short of replacing each of them with one that is known to work (how many people have a spare motherboard lying around?), these codes are the only way of pin-pointing the offender.

Before you can decipher the beep codes, you will need to know the manufacturer of the BIOS chip in your system. The reason for this is that it is the BIOS that produces the beep codes and different BIOS manufacturers use different codes. You will find this information in the PC's documentation. It may also be stamped on the top of the BIOS chip, which is located on the motherboard (see page 17).

Complete lists of BIOS manufacturers' beep codes are available on the Internet.

- AMI beep codes can be found at www.ami.com

- Award beep codes can be found at www.phoenix.com

The following tables show an abbreviated list of the most common beep codes (see margin note).

AMI BIOS	
Beeps	Faulty Device
1, 2 or 3	Memory (RAM). Reseat the module. If that doesn't work, replace it
4 to 7, 9 to 11	Motherboard or expansion card. Remove all the expansion cards; if the system still beeps, the motherboard is faulty. Otherwise, one of the expansion cards is faulty
8	Video system

Note that, on rare occasions, you may not hear any beep codes at all. Assuming the power supply unit is OK, this is a sure sign of a defective motherboard.

Award BIOS	
Beeps	Faulty Device
1	This is normal and indicates that everything is OK
1 long, 2 short	Video system
Any other sequence	Memory

Reseating the CPU has been known to work; it's a long-shot but it might just do the trick.

If the beep codes indicate a motherboard fault, remove all the expansion cards and reboot the PC. If it still refuses to start, then the motherboard or CPU (see margin note) is faulty. If the PC does start, however, one of the cards is faulty. Replace them one by one, rebooting each time until the faulty card is identified.

If you hear no beep codes at all, you almost certainly have a faulty motherboard. This will be confirmed by a dead keyboard (no lights).

With regard to memory modules, if you have just one installed, reseat it; the problem may be a bad connection. If this doesn't work, try moving it to a different slot (it is not unknown for a slot to develop a fault). If that doesn't work either, the module is faulty. However, if you have two, remove one and reboot. If there is still no joy, reinstall it, remove the other one and try again. While it's very unusual, it is possible for a faulty module to prevent the other one from working.

If your PC has both an integrated video system and a video card, you can use one to check the other.

Moving on to video, if you are using a video card, physically remove the card and then replace it to make sure that the connection is good.

If the motherboard has an integrated video system, you can use this to check the video card. All you have to do is connect the monitor to the integrated system and boot the PC. If it starts, you have confirmed what the beep codes were telling you. However, if you are already using the integrated video system, you will have to either replace the motherboard or fit a video card.

Note: text on the boot screen indicates that the video system is OK (with no video, you have no text).

The Hard Drive

Hard drive failure is easy to recognize; the system will get no further than the "Detecting IDE hard drives" stage when it is started. You will see this on the first boot screen immediately after the memory test, as shown below.

Depending on the nature of the problem, you may get an error message as well.

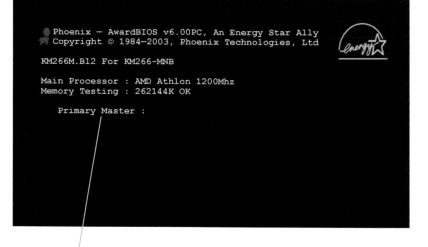

```
 Phoenix — AwardBIOS v6.00PC, An Energy Star Ally
 Copyright © 1984—2003, Phoenix Technologies, Ltd

KM266M.B12 For KM266-MNB

Main Processor : AMD Athlon 1200Mhz
Memory Testing : 262144K OK

    Primary Master :
```

Bootup stops at the "Detecting IDE hard drives" stage

With recent systems, if the drive's model number is not reported (not listed next to Primary Master), there is a problem with the drive itself, its power supply or its connections.

The first thing to check is that the drive is powered up. Open the case and connect a different power plug to the drive. This does two things: it establishes firstly whether or not there is power at the plug and, secondly, that the actual connection is good.

If the drive is listed on the boot screen, it has been recognized by the BIOS. This is a good sign that it is probably OK. This scenario is more likely on older systems and the problem will usually be a configuration issue.

Next, make sure that the interface cable is securely socketed at both ends. If you happen to have a spare one, try using this. If there is still no joy, the drive is faulty.

With older systems, the problem could also be a configuration fault in the BIOS. Carry out the above checks and if they don't resolve the issue, the next thing to investigate is the drive's BIOS configuration. Do this as follows:

Users with an AMI BIOS should go to the Advanced page and then the IDE Configuration page.

1 Enter the BIOS Setup program and open the Standard CMOS Features page. Next to IDE Primary Master, you should see None (if everything was running OK, the drive's model number would be listed here).

```
              Phoenix - AwardBIOS/CMOS Setup Utility
                    Standard CMOS Features

  Date (mm:dd:yy)          Fri, March 26 2006        Item Help
  Time (hh:mm:ss)          14 : 1 : 19

  IDE Primary Master       [None]                   Menu Level
  IDE Primary Slave        [None]
  IDE Secondary Master     [None]                   Press (enter)
  IDE Secondary Slave      [None]                   to enter next
                                                    page for detail
  Drive A                  [1.44MN 3.5]             of hard drive
  Drive B                  [None]                   settings.

  Video                    [EGA/VGA]
  Halt On                  [All Errors]

  Base Memory              640K
  Extended Memory          522346K
  Total Memory             522346K
```

2 Select IDE Primary Master and press Enter. This will open the hard drive Auto-Detection page, as shown below

```
              Phoenix - AwardBIOS CMOS Setup Utility
                    Standard CMOS Features

  IDE HDD Auto-Detection   [Press Enter]            Item Help

  IDE Primary Master       [Auto]                   Menu Level
  Access Mode              [Auto]
                                                    To auto-detect
                                                    the HDD's size,
  Capacity                 400022MB                 head on this
                                                    channel
  Cylinder
  Head
  Precomp
  Landing Zone
  Sector
```

3 Select IDE HDD Auto-Detection and press Enter

The BIOS will now attempt to configure the drive by loading its parameters.

If it succeeds, the drive's parameters will be displayed, as shown below. Save the changes, exit the BIOS and reboot the PC. The problem should now be resolved.

```
                Phoenix - AwardBIOS CMOS Setup Utility
                      Standard CMOS Features

IDE HDD Auto-Detection          [Press Enter]        Item Help

IDE Primary Master              [Auto]           Menu Level
Access Mode                     [Auto]
                                                 To auto-detect
                                                 the HDD's size,
Capacity                        400022MB         head on this
                                                 channel
Cylinder                        19158
Head                            16
Precomp                         7676
Landing Zone                    19157
Sector                          255
```

Hard drive parameters

If the BIOS cannot load the drive's parameters, the drive is faulty and will have to be replaced.

Another problem that can occur is the boot procedure stopping at the "Verifying DMI Pool Data" stage, as shown below.

```
                                        L2 Cache Size    :   64K
Diskette Drive A  : 1.44M 3.5 in        Display Type     : EGA/VGA
Diskette Drive B  : None                Serial Ports     : 3F8
Pri. Master Disk  : None                Parallel Port(s) : 378
Pri. Slave Disk   : None                DDR SDRAM at Bank : 1
Sec. Master Disk  : None
Sec. Slave Disk   : CD-RW, ATA 33

PCI Device Listing ...
Bus No. Device No. Func No. Vendor/Device Class Device Class        IRQ
  0       16        0      1106   3038  0C03  USB 1.0/1.1 UHCI Cntrlr  11
  0       16        1      1106   3038  0C03  USB 1.0/1.1 UHCI Cntrlr  11
  0       16        2      1106   3038  0C03  USB 1.0/1.1 UHCI Cntrlr   5
  0       16        3      1106   3104  0C03  USB 2.0 UHCI Cntrlr       3
  0       17        1      1106   0571  0101  IDE Cntrlr               14
  0       17        5      1106   3059  0401  Multimedia Device         5
  1        0        0      1002   5961  0300  Display Cntrlr           11
                                             ACPI Controller           9

Verifying DMI Pool Data ...
```

This is usually caused by a transient configuration problem that will often be resolved by switching off for a few seconds. If not, it will be a hard drive connection issue that will be fixed by reseating the drive's interface cable connections.

Video

Blank Display

Upgraders probably have more trouble with video cards than any other part of the system. One of the most common problems is installing a new video card and starting the PC up, only to see it stop with a blank screen at the point where Windows is beginning to load.

AGP Aperture Size determines how much of the computer's memory will be available to the video card once its own memory has all been used up.

There are three likely causes of this and they all involve settings in the BIOS.

1) Some BIOSs have a setting which must be set according to the type of video card being used. The default setting is usually PCI, so if you install an AGP card, the setting must be altered accordingly

2) In some PCs that provide integrated video, it will be disabled automatically when a video card is installed. In others, however, it won't be, and this can cause all sorts of problems. In this type of system there will be a BIOS setting that allows the user to disable the integrated video manually

In theory, the AGP Aperture Size should be set to half the amount of installed RAM. In practice, however, this setting sometimes causes problems, in which case a different setting will have to be selected.

3) There is a setting in the BIOS that allows the user to change the AGP Aperture Size (see top margin note) of an AGP video card. This will be set by the computer's manufacturer to a figure that's suitable for the installed AGP card. However, if the user decides to upgrade to a more recent AGP card, it might not work with the existing aperture setting. If this is the case, a blank screen may be the result. The solution, therefore, is to find a setting that will be compatible with the new card. Do this as follows:

Users with an AMI BIOS should go to the Advanced page, Chipset Configuration and then AGP.

1 Enter the BIOS Setup program

2 Select Advanced Chipset Features and press Enter

3 At the next screen, select AGP & P2P Bridge Control

4 Select AGP Aperture Size

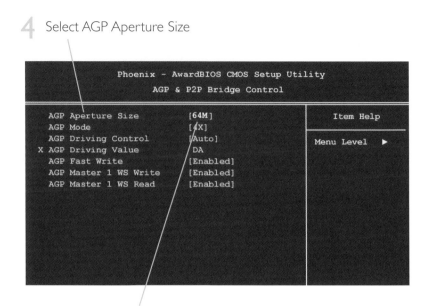

```
         Phoenix - AwardBIOS CMOS Setup Utility
               AGP & P2P Bridge Control

    AGP Aperture Size        [64M]              Item Help
    AGP Mode                 [4X]
    AGP Driving Control      [Auto]          Menu Level    ▶
  X AGP Driving Value         DA
    AGP Fast Write           [Enabled]
    AGP Master 1 WS Write    [Enabled]
    AGP Master 1 WS Read     [Enabled]
```

5 Use the Page Up/Page Down keys to select the [64M] option

Finding the optimum AGP aperture setting is not of critical importance. If your display works at the 64M setting, it's OK to leave it at that.

Return to the main BIOS page, save the change and then exit the BIOS. Reboot the PC and the display should now be restored.

However, finding the *optimum* AGP setting is a matter of trial and error. To do this, keep redoing the above procedure, selecting a higher setting each time, until you find the highest one at which Windows will load.

Resolution/Color Depth Cannot Be Changed

This is a common problem and is a result of the wrong video card driver having been installed. Check this out by right-clicking the Desktop and then Properties, Settings, Advanced. Then click Adapter. The driver currently being used will be shown. If it is the wrong one, click Properties, the Driver tab, and then Update Driver.

A corrupted DirectX driver can also be the cause of a scrambled display. Check this out by installing the latest version.

Scrambled Display

Another problem that can occur when a video card is installed, is being greeted by a scrambled display (an unintelligible mass of colored lines) when the PC is booted. This is usually caused by the monitor's refresh rate being too high. Resolve it as follows:

1 Reboot into Safe Mode (see page 165)

2 When the PC is back in Windows, go to Start, Control Panel, Display. Click the Settings tab and the Advanced button. Then click the Monitor tab

In Safe Mode, Windows will start the PC with a generic "no-frills" video driver that works with all setups.

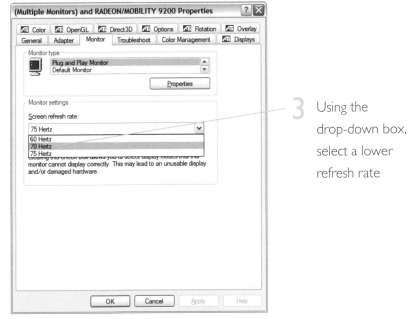

3 Using the drop-down box, select a lower refresh rate

If the refresh rate is too low, it will cause screen flicker, and if it is too high, it will scramble the display.

Flickering Display

A flickering display is caused by a refresh rate that is set too low. Users of Windows XP may find that after installing a new video card (or Windows XP itself), Windows has chosen a very low (often the lowest possible) refresh rate. This results in noticeable screen flicker, which can be extremely irritating.

Resolve it by carrying out step 2 above. Then at step 3, select a higher refresh rate and click OK. The screen will go black for a few seconds and then you'll see a message asking if you want to keep the new setting. If the flickering has gone, click Yes.

Sound

A new sound card has been installed but unfortunately it's not producing any.

One likely cause is that the PC's integrated sound system has not been disabled. Do this as follows:

If your system has an AMI BIOS, go to the Advanced page, Chipset Configuration and then Onboard AC97 Audio.

1 Enter the BIOS Setup program, and on the main page, select Integrated Peripherals

2 Select the "xxx Onchip PCI Device" (xxx is the name of the chipset manufacturer, e.g. Via), and press Enter

3 Find the setting that relates to AC97 Audio and select Disabled

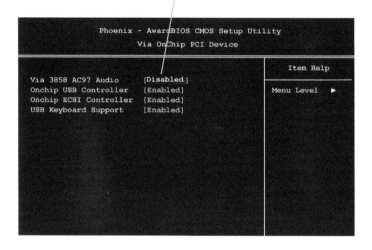

If you have just installed a new CD/DVD drive and aren't getting any sound from it, check that you have connected the drive's audio cable to the PC's sound system (see pages 101–102).

The next thing to check is that the speakers are connected to the sound card and not the integrated system – this is an easy mistake to make.

Then make sure that the speakers are connected to the right jack. This will be stamped as Line Out, Speaker Out or Audio Out.

Check that the speakers are powered up and that volume controls, both on the speakers and in Windows, are turned up.

If there's still no sound, check the sound driver as described on the next page. Finally, check the card's motherboard connection.

Sound system drivers are notorious for corruption. If your PC suddenly loses its sound, the driver is the first thing to check.

In a situation where the sound has been working and then suddenly stopped, suspect the sound system's driver immediately.

1 Go to Start, Control Panel, Sounds and Audio Devices. Click the Audio tab

System Restore is an ideal way of quickly resolving a sound system driver issue.

Sounds and Audio Devices Properties

Volume | Sounds | Audio | Voice | Hardware

Sound playback
Default device:
No Playback Devices
Volume... | Advanced...

Sound recording
Default device:
No Recording Devices
Volume... | Advanced...

MIDI music playback
Default device:
MPU-401
Volume... | About...

☑ Use only default devices

OK | Cancel | Apply

2 If the Sound Playback and Sound Recording boxes are grayed-out then either the driver is corrupted or it hasn't been installed

3 Reinstall the driver to restore the sound

If the driver is OK (indicated by the boxes being active), the problem is hardware-related. Check the speakers and their connections as explained on the previous page.

If the sound is still not working, in the case of an integrated system, the motherboard will need to be replaced. A more practical solution, however, would simply be to buy a sound card.

In the case of a sound card, connect the speakers to the PC's integrated system (after enabling it in the BIOS). If it works now, there is a problem with the sound card. Check that it is securely connected to the motherboard; failing that it will have to be replaced.

Modems

The most common cause of an unsuccessful modem upgrade is installing an incorrect driver. Many modem manufacturers have a habit of supplying driver disks that contain drivers for several different models. This makes it all too easy to install the wrong one.

Dial-Up Modems

If the modem won't dial out, check the following:

Is it installed? Check that it is listed under the Modem category in Device Manager. If it isn't, reinstall the driver from the installation disk. If it still won't dial, you need to dig deeper.

Modem Diagnostic Check. Open Device Manager, locate the modem and right-click it. Select Properties. In the dialog box that opens, click the Diagnostics tab and then click "Query Modem".

AT commands initialize the modem, setting such features as dialing mode (tone or pulse), waits, detection of the busy signal and many others.

1 If you see a list of "AT" commands, this indicates that the modem is working and that the problem is software-related

2 Go back to the Control Panel and click Network Connections. Right-click the modem connection and click Delete

3 Now reinstall the connection. If this was created with a CD from your ISP, then insert the disk and follow the instructions. Alternatively, you can use XP's New Connection wizard

If the modem dials out now, then its software configuration was corrupt. If it still doesn't work, then the modem is almost certainly faulty.

If, however, the AT commands don't appear in the diagnostic test, or you see a "Port Already In Use" message, then the modem is probably using the wrong COM port. Check the modem's documentation to see which port it is designed to use. Then open Device Manager, right-click the modem and select Properties. Click the Advanced tab and then Advanced Port Settings. Check that the modem is set to the right port as per the documentation.

Broadband Modems

You've just installed a modem, hooked it up to your broadband connection, switched on, fired up your browser and ... nothing. All you get is "This page cannot be displayed".

Check the following:

LEDs. All broadband modems have a number of LEDs, each of which indicates something specific. Unfortunately, no two types of modem are the same in this respect so we can't help you on this – you'll need to consult the documentation.

Occasionally, broadband modems will lose contact with the ISP. This can be due to a problem at the ISP's end or to a power outage at the user's end; there are other causes as well. Whatever the cause, the user loses the connection.

The solution to this problem is to "power cycle" the modem. Do it as follows:

Switch the PC off, disconnect the modem and then reconnect it before switching the PC back on. Without going into the reasons, this will re-establish your connection.

Look for the LED that indicates whether or not the modem is receiving data. If it is, this tells you that the ISP's servers are OK, and that the incoming connection to the modem is as well. If not, you know where to look. If you can't find any problems, your ISP's servers are down. Contact them to verify this.

Then check the LED that indicates a good connection between the modem and the PC. If this is out, make sure the cable is plugged in securely at both ends. If you are using a USB modem, check that USB is enabled in the BIOS (see page 63).

Broadband modems need to go through an initialization routine when switched on. With recent modems this takes only a few seconds; older ones, however, may take several minutes. During this procedure, you will not be able to connect to the Internet.

Modem driver. Open the Device Manager and make sure that the modem is listed and that the correct driver has been installed. If not, reinstall it. If there is a warning symbol next to the modem in the list, double-click it to see what the problem is.

Software. Reinstall the ISP's software from the installation disk. If there is still no joy, you should find a diagnostic utility on the installation disk; most ISPs supply one. These utilities can resolve software configuration issues.

As a last resort, you'll have to contact the ISP's technical support.

Monitors

Faults with these devices are very rare. When a fault does occur, it will be either a total failure or some sort of image distortion. Fortunately, particularly in the case of expensive monitors, they can be repaired and there are many repair shops available for this purpose.

Note that CRT monitors carry potentially lethal voltages, and so the average user should never open one up. Troubleshooting, therefore, is restricted to establishing conclusively that the device is faulty – once this is done, take it to a specialist.

With regard to image problems, you don't need a degree to figure this one out. Troubleshooting a blank display isn't too difficult either. The first thing to check (as with all electrical or electronic equipment) is the power supply: if the front panel LED is lit, the device has power; if it isn't, it doesn't have power. In the latter case, check that there is power at the wall socket and that the power cord (including the fuse in the plug) is sound, and firmly connected.

If the LED is lit, the monitor is either in standby mode, in which case pressing the on/off button once will bring it to life, or it is in power management mode. Pressing a key or clicking the mouse should return it to normal operation.

Note that, in some systems, the power management mode may be reluctant to relinquish its grip and a considerable amount of key bashing or mouse clicking may be necessary.

If the screen is still blank, switch off both the PC and the monitor, and then disconnect the VGA or DVI cable from the video system. Switch the monitor back on and if you now see a test signal, as shown left, the monitor is OK; the problem will be with the PC's video system.

Inkjet Printers

A common cause of problems with printers is a transient configuration fault. These can be resolved by the simple expedient of switching off for a few seconds.

If your printer refuses to print anything, your first move should be to switch it off and then back on. Doing so can resolve many configuration issues. If this doesn't work, do the same thing with the PC.

Next, establish whether the fault lies with the printer itself or with the system. This is done with the aid of the printer's test page facility; all printers have one of these.

The procedure varies from printer to printer, so you will have to consult the documentation. Typically, though, it involves isolating the device from the PC by disconnecting the interface cable, powering it up and then pressing a combination of buttons. If the printer is OK, it prints a page full of random characters. You then know that the problem is either a connection issue or software related.

If the test page shows the printer is OK, the first thing to check is that the interface cable is securely connected. If you are using a parallel port printer linked to the PC via another device, such as Zip drive, bypass the device and connect the printer directly (any problems with the other device may interfere with the printer).

Then make sure the printer is correctly installed. Do this by opening Printers and Faxes in the Control Panel; if the device is installed it will be listed here. If it isn't, dig out the driver disk and reinstall it. While you have this window open, make sure that you don't have two or more copies of the driver installed. If you do, delete all of them and then reinstall it.

If you have more than one printer installed, check that the one malfunctioning is set as the default printer (click the device and from the Printer menu, select "Set as default printer").

Finally, check the application that you are printing from, as it is possible for a corrupt program to refuse to communicate with the printer. Type a few lines into Notepad and see if it prints.

Blocked print head nozzles are a common cause of print failure and this is usually caused by lack of use.

If the test page doesn't print, check that the ink cartridges actually contain ink. Then run the head cleaning utility to make sure that the ink nozzles aren't simply blocked with dried ink. This is quite likely if the printer hasn't been used for a while.

Scanners

Problems with scanners, particularly newly installed scanners, are usually related to incorrect connections and power issues.

Parallel Port Scanners

There are two likely problems with these devices:

1) Connecting the scanner to the PC via the "Out" socket. These scanners have two parallel port sockets at the back (as shown below) – one for incoming data and one for outgoing data. You must use the "In" socket

2) Connecting the scanner to the PC via another parallel port device such as a Zip drive or printer. Any problems with the other device will prevent the scanner from working as well

USB Powered Scanners

USB scanners usually draw their power from the USB interface, and as USB can provide only a limited amount, it may be that the scanner is drawing more power than the interface can provide. This will only happen when you have other USB powered devices connected to the system. The temporary solution is simply to disconnect as many of the other devices as necessary. For a permanent fix, you will need to buy an AC powered USB hub, as shown left, that will supply all the power your USB devices need.

Initialization Failure

This is a common problem with scanners and will announce itself with a "Scanner Initialization Failed" error message. There are several causes of this: the scanner hasn't been connected to the system, it isn't powered up or you have selected the wrong driver in the scanning program.

If none of these is causing the problem, however, leave the scanner switched on and reboot the PC. On restarting, very often, the scanner will suddenly be operational.

CD/DVD Drives

Usually, when these devices have a physical problem, the relevant drive icon will be missing in My Computer.

Reboot the PC, and on the first boot screen you should see the drive listed next to Secondary Master. If it isn't, the drive is either faulty or has a connection problem (if it's a newly installed drive, it will probably be the latter). Open the system case and check that the power and interface cables are securely connected. If the interface cable is an older 40-pin cable, try reversing the connection to the drive (it is possible to connect them the wrong way round). If the system still doesn't recognize the drive, it is faulty.

Drive configuration issues relate to the communication channels assigned by Windows that enable the drive to communicate with the CPU. These problems can usually be resolved with the Device Manager.

If the drive is listed on the boot screen but not in My Computer then it has a configuration problem (see margin note). See if the drive is listed in Device Manager and whether any problems are reported there. If so, try the remedy suggested there. Failing that, do the following:

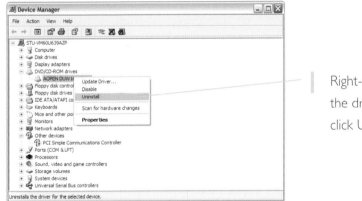

Right-click the drive and click Uninstall

If you have just added a second CD or DVD drive to the system, check that you have configured one as the master and the other as the slave.

2 Switch the computer off and physically disconnect the drive by removing both the power and interface cables. Then reconnect them and reboot. Windows will see the device as a new addition to the system and automatically assign it a new channel, which should resolve the issue.

If the drive isn't listed in Device Manager, follow the procedure described in Step 2 above.

Repair an Under-Performing PC

Buggy, incompatible or corrupted hardware drivers can also cause problems. You should always check the manufacturers' websites for the latest versions and install them. This keeps your hardware up to date and also gets rid of any drivers that have developed problems.

Under-performance in a PC takes several forms. The PC may be unstable and prone to crashing and locking up, it may be unresponsive and generally slow to do what you ask of it, or parts of it may not work at all. These issues can all cause frustration, and in severe cases may even render the PC useless for its intended purpose.

The first thing you need to look at is the amount of software on your machine. The more of it you have, the slower the PC's general performance as the operating system has more to contend with. So your first move is to get rid of as much of it as possible. Go to Add or Remove Programs in the Control Panel and you will see a list of all the applications on your system (you'll probably be surprised at how many you have). Keep the ones you use and uninstall the rest.

Should your system ever start crashing on a periodic basis with a blue error screen, you almost certainly have a faulty RAM module. Replace it as soon as possible.

Maintenance utilities, such as Norton SystemWorks or Nuts & Bolts, are favorite contenders for removal. While these programs can be useful, they do contain applications that are a real drain on the system's resources. Also, be sure to get rid of all freeware and shareware programs you have downloaded from the Internet. These are often written by amateur programmers and can be riddled with bugs.

If you use the Internet a lot, particularly the file-share networks, such as Kazaa, scan your system for the presence of malware (see page 130). For this you will need a suitable program such as Spybot Search & Destroy, a free copy of which can be downloaded from www.safer-networking.org. Run it and you will probably be amazed at the amount of malware it finds. You should also check your system with a virus scanner; viruses can have all sorts of bad effects.

A severely fragmented drive, or one that contains bad sectors, can have a major impact on performance. Run Disk Defragmenter (see page 70) and Chkdsk (see page 165).

Finally, you should reinstall the operating system (see pages 87-90). However, while doing this will repair the many niggling errors that it will have developed over a long period of use, it won't get rid of problems introduced by third-party applications. To do the job properly and return the system to a "like-new" condition, you should do a clean installation. This involves reformatting the hard drive and then reinstalling Windows and all your applications.

Windows XP

We could write a book about troubleshooting Windows XP (in fact, we have: see "Windows XP Troubleshooting in easy steps"), but with just two pages available here, we'll have to restrict ourselves to the biggest fault of all – refusal to start.

When XP has a fault serious enough to prevent it from running (note what we are saying here – faults with XP itself, not other applications preventing it from running), the boot procedure will come to a halt with an error message. There are quite a few of these but the two most common are:

These faults can also be repaired with XP's Recovery Console. This is not an easy way of doing it, however, so do make a point of creating a boot disk.

- System32\config\system File is Missing or Corrupt
- NTLDR is Missing

Either of these error messages indicates that XP's startup files are corrupt, so no matter how many times you reboot, the result will be the same. The solution lies in the form of the boot disk we showed you how to make on page 166. Slip it into the floppy drive, reboot and, as if by magic, XP will start as normal.

Viruses can also be the cause of operating system corruption.

A more serious fault is when XP itself is seriously corrupted. When this happens, bootup stops with a "Disk Boot Failure" error message, as shown below.

```
                                        L2 Cache Size      :    64K

Diskette Drive A  : 1.44M 3.5 in      Display Type      : EGA/VGA
Diskette Drive B  : None              Serial Ports      : 3FB
Pri. Master Disk  : None              Parallel Port(s)  : 378
Pri. Slave Disk   : None              DDR SDRAM at Bank : 1
Sec. Master Disk  : None
Sec. Slave Disk   : CD-RW, ATA 33


PCI Device Listing …
Bus No. Device No. Func No. Vendor/Device Class Device Class        IRQ

    0       16        0      1106   3038   0C03  USB 1.0/1.1 UHCI Cntrlr   11
    0       16        1      1106   3038   0C03  USB 1.0/1.1 UHCI Cntrlr   11
    0       16        2      1106   3038   0C03  USB 1.0/1.1 UHCI Cntrlr    5
    0       16        3      1106   3104   0C03  USB 2.0 UHCI Cntrlr        3
    0       17        1      1106   0571   0101  IDE Cntrlr                14
    0       17        5      1106   3059   0401  Multimedia Device          5
    1        0        0      1002   5961   0300  Display Cntrlr            11
                                                 ACPI Controller            9

Verifying DMI Pool Data ………………
Boot From CD :
DISK BOOT FAILURE, INSERT SYSTEM DISK AND PRESS ENTER
-
```

This error message indicates that the BIOS has been unable to locate the operating system. There are two possible causes for this. The first, as we've already mentioned, is that XP is corrupted beyond recognition, and the second is a faulty hard drive (where the operating system lives).

The hard drive is the first thing to look at (see pages 170-172). If it checks out OK, the problem is with XP and it will need repairing.

The Repair option will remove any updates you have previously installed. Updated drivers will also be reverted to their original versions. Some settings, such as network and performance configurations may be reset to their defaults. However, it won't delete your data, installed programs, personal information, or user settings.

Dig out XP's installation disc and make sure the system is set to boot from the CD-ROM drive (see page 88). Put the disk in the drive and reboot. When you see the message saying "Press any key to boot from CD", do so.

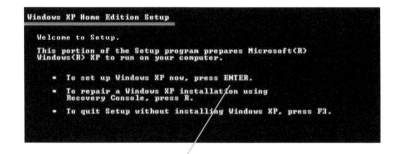

At the first screen, select Set up Windows XP by pressing Enter

At the second, select the Repair Windows XP option by pressing R

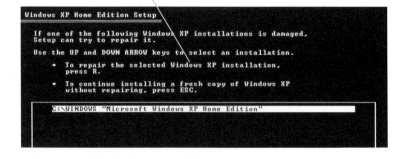

If the XP installation is damaged beyond repair, you will have to reformat the drive and then reinstall XP. The format procedure will wipe the drive clean of all your programs and data. This is the type of situation where a data backup, as described on page 12, will be a life-saver.

The XP installation will now be repaired. However, if you don't see an operating system (highlighted in white), this means that XP has been corrupted beyond repair. Your only option in this case will be to do a new installation.

Index

N

O

P